I-PLAN

MINTCO *FINANCIAL*

mintcofinancial.com

I-Plan

Electronic Book ISBN: 978-0-9855531-0-4

Illustration by Gloria Minter
Book Design by Erik Minter

CREATEMINT°

Made in the U.S.A.

Contents

I-Plan

Featuring:
The Frumpy Family

To all our family, to all our friends, to all my coaches, to all our teachers and to all our homies!

Time to keep it simple and enjoy life making sure our loved ones won't have to go through the same struggles as we have.

I present to you & your family a "road map" of the financial basics that will help keep you on the right track along the entire course of your financial journey and your life overall.

Introduction

Before we get started, I would like to share a little about my background. I grew up in Waldorf, Maryland, which is surrounded by the DMV (District of Columbia, Maryland, Virginia). Growing up in this area, so close to the nation's capital, it seemed that there was always so much to learn and pay attention to. Being aware of the social and economic problems in D.C. helped us learn valuable lessons in our own lives. One thing you needed to learn at a young age was how you could afford new sneakers, and the best brand of jeans, because even though they were expensive it sure felt great to wear them on the first day of school. As we grew older we had to figure out how to save up for video games and laptop computers. Now we are all trying to figure out how to afford the latest tablets, smartphones, TVs, cars that won't break down, nice dinners and well-deserved vacations.

There is so much misinformation out there, we hear it from the media, and now social media, we see it in the out of control antics we see in government. It is getting more difficult to know who is right and who is wrong. We find ourselves asking if it is all just political games or media doom and gloom news. More and more you probably find yourself asking questions like; How can I get a job? How can I secure my job? How can I build a business or work for myself? How much should I be saving or investing or insuring? Where do I need to be financially to enjoy retirement or even get to retirement? With so many things on our plate, and as busy as most of us are, you probably find yourself putting it off. Perhaps you've said "I can get to it another day," or "tomorrow sounds good, doesn't it?" What you should really be thinking is how good you will feel when you've finally tackled your financial issues and how you won't have to worry about it for a long while.

To grow we must continue learning, and we're always learning something new every day of our lives. By focusing on what is most important and showing you what factors you can control, you will easily be able to follow this basic financial roadmap without even needing a GPS.

Going back to my own background, I can remember having my own Kool-Aid drink stands, mowing lawns for $10, cutting hair and learning how to string tennis rackets just to make a few bucks. I tried many different business ventures and while I failed at some, I succeeded with others. My hope with this book is to help you succeed in whatever makes you happy. I want you to never let failure be an option, just realize it is part of your life's learning course.

My own real life experiences came from what we all are faced with each and every day. My beautiful wife Anelise and I continue to learn how to deal with the challenges that many small business owners just like us are up against.

I have helped educate hundreds, if not thousands, of individuals and small business owners over the years, opening their eyes to various financial strategies that have proven successful. Now, I feel that it is time for us to help each other in order to change the direction of our own lives as well as the direction of our country. Within the pages of this book you find a simple financial road map that helps lead you along your financial journey, from the beginning to the end, with a lot of help in between. We call this roadmap the I-Plan.

While reading your way through the roadmap and understanding your I-Plan, you will be creating a financial tool to use when needed. Your I-Plan will help you to enjoy the journey, and to take advantage of the many green nuggets you'll pick up along the way, as well as basic financial fundamentals to help you achieve your own financial freedom. This plan can work for all walks of life and every person who is in need of financial guidance.

Take your time while reading, use the green nuggets of financial knowledge and most importantly, if you come across something that doesn't make sense, is confusing or is something you don't agree with, stop and do a little research on your own. No matter what stage in life you are in, you may feel you know it all when reading, but does your family? Do your kids? Do your parents? Do you, really?

So pass on what you learn, because…

"I Plan, You Plan, We ALL PLAN, with MY I-Plan"

Before starting to learn about the I-Plan, take a moment for yourself. Try to find the most relaxing peaceful place you know in which you can enjoy some ME time, away from noise and the stresses of life. Now close your eyes and look deep within your dreams, and ask yourself what is it that you really want in life, or better yet, what are the things you really need in life? Think about things that are financially related (smartphone, computers, car, career, vacations, education, retirement, house, etc.) anything that costs money to buy or sell. Now think about your life as a whole and the things you cannot place a value or price tag on if you were to lose (health, family, friends, things you enjoy).

Seriously, stop! Don't read any further right now! Enjoy this exercise…hey at least it will give you an excuse to catch up on some sleep, if nothing else.

So often we get caught up in our own lives that we often forget to stop, and refresh our minds in order to appreciate our life's journey and what it really is all about, and ultimately what we really want from life in the end.

Since we were children, we have learned that not everything we want, we can have right away. Some things you have to work hard to be able to get or achieve, and most of the time, it is the best things in life that we have to work so much harder for. Many might even say that the best things in life don't cost a penny, but it's the simple moments in life we need to cherish, such as losing your first tooth and finding money under your pillow in exchange for it, learning to finally ride your bike without coming home scratched and bruised, catching your first fish, getting your first A+, getting your driver's license and driving by yourself, graduating high school, voting for the first time, being old enough to have a beer with your dad, grandpa, or friends, getting in the nightclub with NO X's on your hands because you are now 21, renting your first apartment, getting your first car, ah…the list goes on and on as your life's journey goes on.

Life is GOOD, never forget that, and never forget to enjoy the journey. Remember, it is for you to enjoy and to help you enjoy it fully, you will have the I-Plan in place to keep you on track to achieve success and hold on to the important things in life that really matter.

So now let's make it happen!

◆ Meet The Frumpys ◆

Fred Frumpy	=	Dad
Flo Frumpy	=	Mom
Grandpa & Granny Frumpy	=	Parents of Fred and Flo
Frank Frumpy	=	Son of Fred and Flo
Fran Frumpy	=	Daughter of Fred and Flo
Floyd Frumpy	=	Uncle, Fred's brother
Frida Frumpy	=	Auntie, Fred's sister
Flea	=	Floyd's manager
Fonzie Frumpy	=	You will soon find out more about Fonzie

The Frumpy Family will help you better understand some of the financial issues that you may be experiencing now or might in the future. The Frumpys have financial issues like the rest of us and their story will be helpful to you along your journey to financial freedom.

The Frumpys work, they have a business and like many of us they live paycheck to paycheck. Some of the Frumpys are divorced and some of them have kids. Their kids, like many of our own might want to go to college. They borrow money from their parents and sometimes pay them back. The Frumpys travel to Bahamas and Costa Rica on their credit cards and spend money with no budget in mind. One of the Frumpys is planning to go on a dream cruise someday. The Frumpys want to retire young.

As you can see, the Frumpy Family is faced with the same challenges as any other American family.

When Fred and Flo Frumpy met for the first time, she was working part-time at a diner, to cover her costs for a nursing degree and Fred was working hard to start his own business right out of high school. Grandpa Frumpy wanted Fred to be a doctor. But plans changed as they often do.

Fred and Flo got married somewhat under pressure, because Flo became pregnant at the age of 18 and Granny Frumpy was very upset with the situation. However, it did turn out to be a beautiful wedding. This was just the beginning of their journey.

Soon the Frumpy's daughter was born and they named her Francine. The Frumpys were amazed at how fast little Francine grew.

Francine, who became known as Fran, also proved to be a good distraction for Granny and Grandpa Frumpy, while her Auntie Frida was going through a divorce.

Auntie Frida decided that she got tired of her hubby and high school sweetheart, Flea.

Flea is the manager and trainer of Uncle Floyd, who is a professional fighter. He is a celebrity and can date any woman he wants. One day, Frank Frumpy was at Uncle Floyd's house and guess who was there? The beautiful actress Fofina! He could not believe it!

Confused? Sometimes they are too, but the Frumpys are here to help you see your financial troubles and solutions to those troubles more clearly.

Chapter I

Need vs Want

NEED

What is a need?

A need is something you have to have; it is something you can't live without.

A need would be something like food or water. You need food and water to survive.

WANT

What is a want?

A want is something you would like to have. It is not absolutely necessary, but it would be nice to have.

A want can be so many things. It might be the latest computer, tablet, smartphone, purse, shoes or 60" television, and the list can go on and on.

So how do you figure out your own set of needs and wants?

Each person is different and has a different set of needs and wants. But if you think in terms of basics, our "Needs" are very similar to everyone else's because we all need the same things to stay alive. What really differs are our "Wants."

Now that you know the difference between wants and needs, you will next learn how important that difference is and be able to build a "healthy pocket." This pocket will give you full control of your financial life, both now and in the future.

So let's determine what you "Need" and what you "Want."

Many things we wish for are not really as important as we

make them seem to be or are even necessary to live our lives.

Stop and take a few minutes to ask yourself the following questions. Do you think upgrading your phone plan is really necessary? Or buying a new watch, chain, earrings or more bling? Or getting the latest and greatest out-of-this world smartphone? Are all of these things necessary?

I hope you have heard this story many times, but if not it's about time you wake up to the realities of life. While these types of things may not be necessary to live your life, you don't want to be out of the norm compared to what your friends might have. We all want to fit in at school, work, and in society. We all want to look good, feel good, and feel special and successful. My parents often used to say, "Stop trying to keep up with the Joneses." Not sure who the Joneses were then or who the Joneses are these days, but you know what I mean. You can see it on MTV or TMZ or ESPN or any other channel that people tune into to find out what is "in" and what is "out," or what is hip or fashionable right now.

For now, just keep in mind that in order to achieve the success you desire, you need a plan. A plan for your pocket, that's right, this plan will get you headed on the right track.

The best part of having an I-Plan is that YOU are in full control.

So it will be YOU that will take action and it will be YOU that will be rewarded.

Now it is time to tackle your own set of wants and needs. To start, you will have to figure out what you

NEED and what you WANT.

NEEDS

_____
_____
_____
_____
_____
_____
_____
_____
_____
_____
_____
_____
_____
_____
_____
_____
_____
_____
_____
_____
_____
_____
_____
_____
_____
_____
_____
_____

WANTS

_____
_____
_____
_____
_____
_____
_____
_____
_____
_____
_____
_____
_____
_____
_____
_____
_____
_____
_____
_____
_____
_____
_____
_____
_____
_____
_____
_____

To make it clear and easy, take a sheet of paper and make two columns; one will be your needs and the other will be your wants.

In the needs column write down all things that cost money out of your pocket and have to be paid in order for you to live and work properly.

In the wants column you list all of the items or activities you want but are not a necessity to your life. For example:

Needs	Wants
Food and Water	Car
Money (or income)	Cable TV
Home	Phone
Utilities (water, gas, electric)	Toys
Insurance	Gifts, Movies, Restaurants
	Travel

Please be very specific, and list everything you can think of. You might think that the coffee you buy in the morning is a necessity for you to keep going during the work day and extra hours at the office. So list it as a need! Why not?

When you're finished take a few minutes to look back on the lists and reflect. Ask yourself the following questions, and most importantly be honest with yourself as you answer them.

Why do you feel these things are necessary?
What things do you want?
Why do you want these things?
Are any of your wants also needs? If so write them down.

The Frumpys on the I-Plan

Fran is a true fashionista!!! She loves shopping with her mom, Flo. The problem is that she has very expensive taste. She wants handbags from Fouis Futton, earrings from Fartier, the list goes on and on.

Fred Frumpy is a good business man and a caring dad, and so he told his daughter Fran she needs to first learn what wants and needs are and what the difference between them is before he would buy her anything more. Of course, she did not under-stand why.

Fred said, "Fran, just do it and I will explain it later, you'll see."

Here is what Fran wrote down for her own list of "Wants" and "Needs":

Fran's Wants:

Handbag by Fouis Futton
Earrings by Fartier
Dress by FERA
Shoes by FF
Smartphone 5F
Dinner and movies every Friday night

Fran's Needs:

Gasoline (to drive to her job at FrumpySoft)
Car Insurance
Food
Rent Money

Chapter II

Napkin on the Fridge

Now that you have the list of needs and wants, it is time to review this list and build your budget! You knew I was going to talk about a BUDGET, right?

Yes, we do have to talk about a budget.

How many times have you heard the word "budget?" Hearing the word is sometimes just as tiring as hearing your mom telling you to eat your vegetables. And she was right, so we had better start listening to her wisdom. We hear it all the time, everywhere. From politicians going on and on about budgets to the media going on and on about how bad our budgets are. Even our parents asking if we budgeted for that new pair of shoes we were planning to buy. So, really, what's so important about the word "budget?"

It is very difficult today to take politicians, the media and sometimes our own parents, too seriously when it comes to budgets, because they often act as though theirs is unlimited. The reality is that our budgets are NOT. So all of us that have to put on our armor each morning and go to school and/or work, we can't even start to think about getting ahead in life if we don't have a budget to follow.

Doesn't the word "budget" sound overwhelming just thinking about it? Have you taken the time to do one? Maybe you have, but just haven't looked at yours in a while, because you're too nervous to see what you really might have to cut, or think there is too much work and time involved versus spending that time and energy doing more fun things like hanging out with family or friends, talking on the phone, playing on the computer, watching television or any other activity you enjoy.

I am sure, when asked if you have a budget, most of you usually say "Oh we'll figure it out when my paycheck comes." Yeah sure, you'll figure it out and that's probably why you are reading this book! Today is the day you will do your budget so you don't have to figure it out the hard way, when it's too late. When you're broke it ain't no joke. I'm sure you've heard one of those sayings or have had that feeling before.

So I will keep it very simple for you, how about we just throw out the intimidating word "budget," and simply call it "Napkin on the Fridge."

Sounds much more simple and doable, right?

"Napkin on the Fridge"

We are going to make it that easy, so there are NO EXCUSES. Get a magic marker and a napkin, yes this is really all you need! Take just 10 minutes to write your budget on the napkin using the following form as a guide. It seriously only takes 10 minutes! Once you have finished your budget, post your napkin on the fridge and this is where it will stay.

Monthly Income NEEDS

Primary Residence	
Mortgage or Rent	$
Property Insurance	$
Umbrella Policy	$
Property Taxes	$
HLOC or Mortgage	$
Utilities	$
Cables/Satelite TV	$
Internet Service	$
Telephone	$
Cell Telephone	$
Routine Maintenance	$
Yard Services	$
Pool Services	$
Major Repairs	$
Other	$
Other	$
Other	$
Primary Residence Total	$

Health & Medical	
Medical Insurance	$
Dental Insurance	$
Medicare Premiums	$
Medical RX Premiums	$
RX out-of-pocket	$
Other out-of-pocket	$
Other	$
Other	$
Medical Total	$

Food & Clothing	
Groceries	$
Drugstore Non-RX	$
Hardware	$
Clothing	$
Dry Cleaning/Laundry	$
Other	$
Other	$
Food, Clothing Total	$

Transportation	
Auto Loan/Lease	$
Auto Loan/Lease	$
Gasoline	$
Maintenance	$
Auto Insurance	$
Auto Registration Fees	$
Other	$
Transportation Total	$

Insurance & Misc.	
Life Insurance & Premium	$
LTD Insurance Premium	$
LTC Insurance Premium	$
Other	$
Other	$
Other	$
Misc Total	$

Primary Residence Total	$
Health & Medical Total	$
Food & Clothing Total	$
Transportation	$
Insurance Total	$
Insurance & Misc Total	$
Monthly Total Income Need	$

Monthly Income WANTS

Vacation Residence	
Mortgage or Rent	$
Property Insurance	$
Umbrella Policy	$
Property Taxes	$
HLOC or Mortgage	$
Utilities	$
Cables/Satelite TV	$
Internet Service	$
Telephone	$
Cell Telephone	$
Routine Maintenance	$
Yard Services	$
Pool Services	$
Major Repairs	$
Other	$
Other	$
Other	$
Vacation Residence Total	$

Family & Misc	
Church Donations	$
Charitable Donations	$
Family Assistance	$
Gifts for Family	$
Gifts for friends	$
Other	$
Other	$
Family & Misc. Total	$

Entertainment	
Restaurants	$
Hobbies	$
Sporting Event Tickets	$
Club/Membership Dues	$
Movies/Shows/Concerts	$
Other	$
Other	$
Entertainment Total	$

Travel	
Tickets	$
Gasoline	$
Hotels	$
Food	$
Shopping	$
Activities & Entertainment	$
Other	$
Travel Total	$

Primary Residence Total	$
Health & Medical Total	$
Food & Clothing Total	$
Transportation	$
Insurance Total	$
Insurance & Misc Total	$
Monthly Total Income Want	$

Fred Frumpy told Fran to fill out the same form. She needs a "Napkin on the Fridge" URGENTLY! What she earns at FrumpySoft is not covering her expenses, and she needs to realize this quickly! If she doesn't, she's going to have to start thinking about having a garage sale in order to pay her bills.

Chapter III

Napkin on the Fridge x Wants & Needs

Once you fill out the "Napkin on the Fridge" form, your next step is to compare it with the list of wants and needs that you made earlier.

This should be interesting! Now that it's in black and white it's probably easier to see with your own eyes. Now, is it good news or is it worrisome?

Are you in the Red or in the Green?

In the Red means you are creating debt.

In the Green means you are creating GREEN Moolah...
Money...Equity...Cash...Dinero...
YES!!! It is so very NICE to be in the Green.

In the financial world, people say you are "in the money" when you are in the Green and "out of the money" when you are in the Red. It's not easy these days to be in the Green, so pat yourself on the back, smile, kick back and say "I love to be GREEN," because you deserve it.

And for those of you in the RED, no worries, that's why you are reading this book. We all are continually living and learning, and it's NEVER too late to start changing your ways. So get started and make today a day to digest new information and start tomorrow as a new day with a changed way of how you do things.

In fact, you can even take that "Napkin on the Fridge" and stick it in the garbage can instead if you want, because tomorrow will be the day you figure out how to get it on the Fridge, and be a "Born Again Green Machine."

Remember, there are some things that are really not as important as you think (your wants). The good news is that much of what you may want can be reduced or even cut from your "Napkin on the Fridge" until you reach a number you can live comfortably with, while knowing you have some extra money available for an emergency fund (also known as Rainy Day fund).

Now, back to Fran Frumpy. Fran is in the RED! She knows she has to cut some of her wants to be able to be in the Green. That means no more shopping for Fartier earrings for a while.

Chapter IV

Checking Account

Once you start staying in line with your "Napkin on the Fridge" you will find you have some money at the end of the month, so what do you do with it?

The first thing you want to do is interview a few local banks.

Wear something nice like a suit and tie if you're a man or skirt suit if you're a woman. You'll want to dress and carry yourself as though you are going for a job interview. You will also need to bring a list of questions with you.

That's right...you are going to be interviewing the bank! It's about time you realize that banks need us just as much as we need them.

So you want to go into your bank interview prepared to consider the following:

Is this the kind of bank that you want to work with?

Are they going to appreciate your business?

Do you need a bank that provides a physical location or do you just need online banking services?

It is also important to realize there are many banks competing for your business, so feel confident in knowing that you are the boss of your money, and you want your money to be treated just as important as the bank employees treat their boss.

Now that you are looking great and feeling confident and have some money to open a checking account, you need to determine the following:

1. What is the purpose of the account (online banking, check deposits, check cashing, or ATM usage)?
2. How much do they charge in fees for each of the services listed above?
3. Are there transaction fees, if so, for what type of usage, and how much?
4. Can you have an overdraft protection added to the account? If so, how much does it cost and are there any other associated fees? Also, make sure to ask if they can provide a minimum overdraft protection amount of $500, this will help protect you in the future against any unnecessary fees or payments that you may miscalculate for.
5. Last but not least, does this bank offer FREE CHECKING? If so, you need to find out if there is a minimum balance you must have in the account so that you are not charged a fee. Also, find out if, as a new client, the bank will provide you a box of free checks. Many banks will send you promotional gifts you will never use, need, or want, so instead you will want to ask them to waive the complimentary gift and ask for a box of free checks instead.

If you feel like you might forget some of these important questions, go ahead and write them down and take them with you. Feel free to add your own questions or concerns about other services the bank might offer.

After interviewing at least three banks, take your time to compare each bank carefully, keeping in mind all fees or costs associated with opening a checking account at each one. If you plan on using the bank primarily for ATM usage, make sure the bank will waive withdrawal fees at any

ATM, or determine if that bank has ATMs conveniently available in all of the places you think you will most likely be withdrawing money from.

Remember it's your money, and you know how easy it can come and go. So be sure before deciding on a checking account, the bank answers all your needs and addresses all of your wants and concerns. Most importantly make sure the bank doesn't nickel and dime you when it comes time to getting your money. You may even want to consider an online bank, but just make sure it is reputable and is FDIC (Federal Deposit Insurance Corporation) insured. They may have lower fees for the type of banking you will be doing, and if you are one who prefers to pay all your bills online, this may be an ideal approach to your banking needs.

You are the boss of your money, and remember there is always another bank across the street or online that you can take your money to.

Fran went to a local bank hoping to open a free checking account. Fran's father made sure he taught her how to negotiate. The bank manager knew Mr. Frumpy and agreed to give Fran a No-Fee checking account as long as she agrees not to go over her limit. For this reason, they did not provide over-draft protection on her checking account, which means she will always have to be careful of going into the RED with her purchases, because each time she does she will have to pay a fee.

Chapter V

Assets/Liabilities

Knowing the difference between assets and liabilities might seem like a basic exercise, but reinforcing this is vital for sticking to your "Napkin on the Fridge" and following your I-Plan to financial freedom. This understanding is important in life to help you evaluate what you are truly worth. Doing this exercise requires you to take the assets that you own and subtract your liabilities; this will tell you how much you are truly worth.

I bring this up because we often see or read about celebrities and athletes making a great deal of money. Or you might have a friend or neighbor with the nicest car or biggest house. Like the good ole' cliché says, "don't judge a book by its cover." These people might make a lot of money or seem like they do, but without knowing their "Napkin on the Fridge" it can be hard to tell what they are actually worth. Many times, these people don't even know their budgets or whether they are in the green or red. This is the reason why we always see so many articles written about how these celebrities and athletes went broke.

If you have more liabilities than assets, that means you TOO are broke, but no worries we are going to change that, right?

Assets = things that will make you money, appreciate, hold value over time or create passive income.

Liabilities = things that do not make you money, depreciate, lose value over time, or may be worthless or have no value when you go to sell.

Take a moment to think about things that are assets and liabilities.

Examples:
Assets = cash, gold, investments, property

Liabilities = credit card debt, mortgage, car loans, clothing, boats, TVs, phones, computers, gadgets (oh of course some of these things are a lot of fun, but where do they normally end up?)

So now that you have a pretty good understanding of how assets and liabilities differ, let's move on to get an even better understanding of how you create liabilities for yourself.

Since we are talking about celebrities, we have to talk about Floyd Frumpy. Floyd Frumpy is a professional fighter and over the years has made a ton of money.

With every fight, Floyd envisions all of the gold and bling he will buy and all of the money going to his bank account. He has bought many powerful cars, mansions and expensive toys. He is a wonderful uncle with a huge heart. He likes to give gifts to everyone, including his darling, the beautiful actress Fofina. Uncle Floyd has no limits on his money and says he can always make more.

But what are his assets and liabilities, really?

Uncle Floyd's Assets are:

Cash, investments and properties; but are they in his name?

Uncle Floyd's Liabilities are:

Cars, boats, clothing, expensive travels, TVs and of course, Fofina's luxury purchases.

Fofina is Uncle Floyd's girlfriend, or one of them anyway. She always is demanding for him to give her a new car, more plastic surgery and pay for trips for her whole family. Aside from all that, she has an unlimited credit card in Uncle Floyd's name.

Flea, Uncle Floyd's manager, told Floyd to look for a good, professional financial advisor, not one of his boys or so-called friends.

Looking from the outside in, many people would

think Uncle Floyd doesn't need financial advice with all the money he makes. Flea knows everything about Uncle Floyd, so why would he tell Uncle Floyd to get a good financial advisor? Judging by the way Uncle Floyd lives, how could his financial life be a mess?

For some reason he says "there is always another Pay Day."

Chapter VI

Credit/Debt

This should be considered one of the most important chapters, please take the time to read it and understand it, and if you still have questions ask someone who knows a lot about finances or do some research on your own.

Someone said to me once, "You can't take a withdrawal, without a deposit."

To better understand, you first must know what "credit" is and what a "debt" is.

It is very simple:

Credit is the ability to obtain goods or services before needing to pay for them. This is based on the trust or goodwill that payment will be paid back in the future in full, most likely with interest (interest is how the lender makes money). You borrow from a person or business to receive goods, service or money NOW, establishing an IOU or credit, in which you will be obligated to pay back for such items in the future, usually with interest.

IOU = If someone agrees to receive equivalent value later in exchange for his/her goods, he/she has accepted an IOU. An IOU is a credit for the seller and a debt for the buyer. If the IOU becomes negotiable, meaning others will accept it in exchange for goods and services, the IOU has value. Debt is very similar; however it is what you own. Debt is something owed, such as money, goods or services. Let's understand the difference between credit and debt.

If you have credit you will be able to purchase things that you may not be able to pay in full today, but in the future. How about a television for example? Let's say you like this brand new television that costs $1,000, but you don't have $1,000 in cash. However, you would be able to pay $1,000 over the next 12 months, so you might consider applying for credit with the store that is selling the television. This can be very risky, because remember the place you are buying from will make money on what? That's right! The sale and the institution lending you the money will make money on the interest they charge you. Many times the store that is selling the television will offer a deal, ZERO INTEREST for the next 12 months, in the hopes that you miss one payment.

Now before reading any further, always remember this green nugget:

"IF IT SOUNDS TOO GOOD TO BE TRUE, IT USUALLY IS!"

So always look at the FINE PRINT, read the contract or agreement and ASK QUESTIONS to see if there is a catch.

Think about it, you can buy this hot new television, for $1,000 at ZERO interest, and pay it in full over the next 12 months. That looks good when you put that on your "Napkin on the Fridge" and you're still in the Green every month, doesn't it? Especially knowing you are going to have the nicest TV imaginable, right?

Well the truth is, if you fail to make one of those payments, or pay one late you are going to be in big trouble. That ZERO percent interest agreement you made, you can bet your lunch, will be GONE with the wind. Your interest will more than likely be as high as 20% going forward. WOW! Think about that for a moment, that's almost 2 more payments ($1,000 x .20= $200). Wam...Bam...Thank You, Ma'am! You read that right, $200 more. You were given credit for $1,000 and thanks to one missed or late payment, you now will be in debt for $1,200.

You own the debt, even though you were given the credit, you now own the debt that is $1,200 or more, pending the fine print, all because of one missing payment. Also, your minimum payment will increase each month from here on. The lesson here is always be sure read the fine print, no matter what your smooth-talking sales person tells you.

Just think, you only missed one payment, imagine if you missed two payments. If you did this, you would have to expect to lose any future credit and the ability to purchase other things on credit with the same store or any other business. If you missed too many payments, you could also expect some big scary dudes to knock on your door saying, "Open Up, we are here to take your hot, top-of-the-line TV back." You read that right, you will not only lose your credit, but you can also expect to lose that TV as well. After all, the bank or institution who provided you the credit/loan would rather sell the TV to someone for cash in their pockets, than have someone owe money on it; especially someone who isn't paying anything towards the credit/loan.

So be wise, when you first start establishing credit. For decades, Americans have had the opportunity to get things by having good credit. However, after the nationwide real estate crisis in 2008 and the current credit crisis, many people lost not only their jobs and homes, but also their good credit. Since then, qualifying to purchase things on credit has become even more difficult and banks have raised their requirements, or the qualifications you need to meet in order to get the bank to lend you money. They have made it very difficult to establish "New Credit," or any credit at all. Be wise, always turn to your "Napkin on the Fridge" and think hard about what you are buying and really take the time to consider if it is really wise to use credit vs. good old, reliable cash to buy something. Most importantly take time to seriously consider if what you want to buy is a need or a want.

So why do you need credit anyway?

You need credit to purchase things you do not have cash to pay in full or money available right away, but you are able to pay in full over a period of time, even with interest. Always ask what the interest rate is and calculate what the interest will cost you, before establishing credit for anything you are planning to buy using credit.

By now you should have a pretty good understanding of the differences between assets and liabilities. Now you can move on and continue learning. If you're still a bit confused, stop here and go back a chapter.

Is there such a thing as a good debt?

Yes, a good debt is an investment that in time can make you money.

Starting a business or buying an asset that will appreciate, or in other words increase in value over time, can be a good debt.

A good philosophy you should try to live by is, "only borrow money when it is going to make you money over time."

Let's look to the Frumpy Family for an example.

Granny Frumpy is a real estate investor. She owns

many properties in South Florida. All of her properties are rentals. Granny Frumpy always tells the family the same old story about how she started her business.

In the beginning, Granny Frumpy did not have a good credit history, so she borrowed money from her rich cousin and bought her first property with that money. The first property she purchased was a boarding house that generated very good cash flow for her from the payments the renters paid her.

Granny Frumpy's second property, like many other properties she bought later on, she purchased using borrowed money from her bank. She was able to do this because, Granny Frumpy was smart and she built her credit history up by paying her cousin on time and kept all the documents to prove that she did. This helped Granny Frumpy qualify for a loan on her properties. She was smart because she had enough money in rent payments coming in each month to pay her loan back to the bank as well as the expenses of maintaining her properties. She borrowed the money from the bank because she did not have the full amount of money available to buy the properties outright with cash when she first started.

Granny knew she had a debt – but it was a good debt because in the long term, she paid it off, and now she is collecting the rent payments, but not having to pay anyone back for money she borrowed. Aside from maintenance expenses, the money is all Granny's.

With her continually good cash flow, Granny Frumpy decided to help her son Fred Frumpy start his own business, called FrumpySoft, a technology company that sells management software.

Granny Frumpy's good debt generated enough cash flow to pay off her existing debt with the bank and was able to invest in a new business for her son Fred.

You might say, "Wow! This Granny is quite a savvy business woman!" And you'd be right!

Chapter VII

Building Credit

You can start building your credit by applying for a credit card. Make sure you always pay your balance in full and on time. This way you can easily start to build your credit history properly. Often times, when applying for credit for the first time, the company issuing you the card will require you to secure the amount you are applying for with cash.

This is done to make sure you start using your credit wisely, and you do not use up all your credit and then run off to another country while the lender is left high and dry. It's almost like you are borrowing from yourself. So the company who issues you the card knows that if you run off without paying your credit card bill, they will at least have the money you originally secured the card with.

Another way to build your credit is to make a purchase from a store that offers credit and apply for a credit card for your purchase from that store. It is important to always keep in mind that should you make a bad decision by not paying the credit bill due or continually make late payments you will be destroying any credit you have now or any credit you could have had in the future.

Regardless of how you approach starting to build your credit, start slowly and only apply for amounts that you can handle, or better yet not even use up completely. One idea for building credit is to use a credit card only for fueling up your car and making sure you pay off the balance completely each month.

Let's see how one of the Frumpy's builds his own credit. Frank Frumpy started to build his credit history when he applied for a Future-MART credit card in order to buy his first TV.

So far he has paid all of his payments in full and on time. He is building a good credit history and protecting his credit.

This means that in the future, he can apply for a larger amount and maybe even buy his first rental property like Granny Frumpy. Maybe he'll choose to use it to buy his first car. Frank's dad Fred probably won't buy Frank a car because he believes it is important to teach both Fran and Frank the important lesson about the value of money, and there is no better way to do this than by having them learn on their own through experience.

Chapter VIII

Protecting Your Credit

Think of your credit as your financial health. Take good care of it, nurture it, and make sure it will be around for you to enjoy for the rest of your life.

To protect your credit you need to make sure you pay all of your bills on time. Most importantly, you should try your hardest to stay out of consumer debt (think back to your "wants" list). This means only buying things you can pay for now or have saved money for specifically. The bottom line is, only buy what you can afford. This is also called living within your means. While nothing is wrong with having some "wants," such as a nice trip with your friends or a fancy new car, you just have to plan ahead and save for it. You will learn in time that the better you protect your credit, the more opportunities you will have to use it wisely as it increases. Keep in mind that once you lose it, it will take many years to restore it.

Protecting your credit is just as important as building it. Paying your bills on time will help you build good credit while protecting it. Keep the following dos and don'ts in mind to help ensure you keep your credit protected. Do not give your Social Security number (SSN) or similar personal information to anyone. Be careful when you buy things online, do not give too much information to online retailers and be sure the site offers secure online transactions. Do not carry passwords for accounts or your Social Security card in your wallet. The last thing you want is to one day find out that you have a "long lost" brother or sister who just happens to have the same exact name and address as you but is living in another country.

What is a credit report?

A credit report is a record of your credit activities. It lists any and all credit card accounts or loans you may have, the balances of each loan and how regularly you make your payments. It also shows if any action has been taken against you because of unpaid bills.

Ideally, you should check your credit report with each of the following three credit bureaus: Equifax, Trans Union, and Experian. You should check your report once a year or when considering making a large purchase. Did you know that you are entitled by law to one free copy of your credit report from each of these three credit bureaus once a year? It's true! So you might as well take advantage of it.

A credit report is very important, because many companies review your credit history in order to determine if they want to do business with you. That's why it is so important that you pay ALL of your bills on time, ALWAYS.

For those of you that really want to have a "healthy pocket" you should strongly consider only using credit to buy assets and not liabilities.

Chapter IX

Emergencies Cash Reserves
aka "Rainy Day Account"

I can't tell you how many times I have heard, "Hey, I want to start investing so I can make a lot of money."

My response is almost always, "Sounds good let's start tomorrow, but what if you lose your job? Will you need this investment to support yourself, family, or to pay your bills? Do you have an Emergency Fund or reserve?"

Just remember that you are only ready to invest money when you are ready to lose money. You might be thinking, isn't that like gambling? Well, yes, it is like gambling in a way. But we'll discuss later in our financial journey.

For now, let's look at the importance of having a cash reserve or emergency fund, and why it's so important to have it established before thinking about investing, buying a home, or starting a retirement account.

An emergency fund is money you set aside for emergency situations ONLY. Some people choose to call these rainy days instead of emergencies.

What are rainy days?

Rainy days are those days or months when you can't find a job or maybe you just lost your job. These might be days where you had a medical emergency, or your car broke down. Rainy days can be any situation you can think of that occurs unexpectedly and is going to cost you some serious pennies or maybe hundreds of dollars.

There are many emergency situations you can call rainy days, and to prepare for these situations you have to build a cash reserve now. Otherwise you will not be able to pay your bills and your credit will begin to sink as fast as the Titanic (I'm sure you know the story).

How much should I save for rainy days?

First you should take a look at your "Napkin on the Fridge" and see which of your expenses are "needs." Now multiply the total sum of your needs by six (the six is for 6 months). It's that simple. Many agree that three months of your total income, or 25% of your yearly income, should be in an emergency cash reserve. So again, to keep things simple and always be a little ahead of the curve, just pull out your "Napkin on the Fridge" and multiple your needs by six. The equation is 6 x your needs = your emergency cash reserve.

Isn't that simple? In theory yes, but in real life, it's up to you to take ACTION and put this theory into practice in order to begin establishing your "rainy day" or emergency fund account.

You should also consider opening a line of credit with your bank and leave it open and unused, just in case you need it for that unexpected emergency. This type of account is not always easy to obtain and will depend an your "Napkin on the Fridge," but if you can find a bank that is willing to give you a line of credit, take advantage of it and keep it open.

However, don't forget that this account is only to be used as an emergency fund. Don't allow yourself to dip into it for everyday expenses when there is no emergency. It is to only be used when there is nothing more you can do with your "Napkin on the Fridge," meaning there is no more that you can cut from your budget, it's the last resort. If nothing else, just remember it is not a vacation fund or "mad money" account.

Where should my cash reserve/emergency fund be kept?

You want to make sure it's in a savings account that is liquid at all times, and will always be there when you need it. This will reduce the risk that it will lose any of its value and can be accessible at all times. You can keep this account with your current bank or another bank that might give you a better interest rate. But, remember we are not concerned with making money on this account; we are most concerned with it being SAFE, meaning it won't lose value, and LIQUID, which means it is available for withdrawal at any time.

Don't forget about credit unions. They are another great place to start building your cash reserve/emergency fund.

Credit unions are non-profit cooperative financial institutions owned and operated for the benefit of their members. Credit unions fill a role similar to that of banks, as they both take in deposits and make loans. However, because they operate on a non-profit basis (and are generally exempt from taxes paid by banks), they tend to offer higher rates of interest on deposits and lower rates of interest on loans than for-profit banks do. Earnings may be returned to members as dividends.

Check in your local community if there are any credit unions that would work well for your particular situation.

Also, don't forget to review various online banking institutions that are FDIC insured. They may offer better rates and may provide as easy access to your money based on your needs.

Time to check back in with the Frumpys.

When Auntie Frida divorced Flea, she was working as a hotel manager at a resort in Costa Rica. What a nice place to be! That's when she got tired of Flea. Imagine the opportunities she saw on the beach, all those hot surfers and... well you get the point. Some might say she was "living the life," much like Uncle Floyd, the successful fighter you met earlier.

Auntie Frida had no clue that Flea had protected himself against divorce. Flea always thought Uncle Floyd was going to be a champion and their lives would change financially someday. So Flea made sure he and Frida made a pre-nuptial agreement before getting married. Because of this, Auntie Frida did not get anything but their house when they did divorce.

Frida never did build an emergency fund or even have a "Napkin on the Fridge." Throughout their marriage Flea paid all of their expenses and he had control of their "Napkin." After the divorce, Frida spent all of her earnings on her surfer studs, bubbles and boards. What a life!

Auntie Frida kept working in Costa Rica after the divorce, but she had to break up with the boys because that life was getting expensive. Frida now had to concentrate on building her "Napkin on the Fridge," or she would be living under a bench on the beach. Now that's not the life any of us want.

The good news is that she is now working on building up her emergency fund and is planning on setting up a retirement fund. She was able to do this after she learned the valuable life lessons of financial freedom.

Granny and Grandpa Frumpy would not help her financially, because they always felt it was important she learn the hard way on her own, so she could someday be independent and truly appreciate the value of money.

Chapter X

The Value of Money

You've been learning a lot, so let's take a break to sing with John Lennon:

The best things in life are free
But you can tell me 'bout the birds and bees.
Now gimme money (that's what I want)
That's what I want (that's what I want)
That's what I want, ye-ye-yeh,
That's what I want.

Money don't get everything its true.
What it don't get I can't use.
So gimme money (that's what I want)
A little money (that's what I want)
That's what I want, ye-ye-yeh,
That's what I want.

Yeh gimme money (that's what I want)
A little money (that's what I want)
That's what I want (that's what I want)
So gimme money (that's what I want)
That's what I want, ye-ye-yeh,
That's what I want.

Your lovin' give me a thrill
But your lovin' don't pay my bill.
Now gimme money (that's what I want)
That's what I want (that's what I want)
That's what I want, ye-ye-yeh,

That's what I want.
Money don't get everything its true.
What it don't get I can't use.
So gimme money (that's what I want)
A little money (that's what I want)
That's what I want, ye-ye-yeh,
That's what I want.

Yeh gimme money (that's what I want)
A little money (that's what I want)
That's what I want (that's what I want)
So gimme money (that's what I want)
That's what I want, ye-ye-yeh,
That's what I want

We need money to pay for our needs and wants. Money is a part of everyone's life. But what is the real value of money?

Money is valuable because we want it, but we want it only because it can get us a product or service or any number of other things we enjoy.

Many of us have learned throughout life that for us to get money, we need to work for it. One thing I have personally learned is that people, who work hard for their money, are the people that value it the most. I guess because they know how hard it is to come by and we all know money sure doesn't grow on trees.

The foundations and principles that each of us hold, came from what our parents taught us when we were kids and as we grew into adults. If you had parents that gave you everything easily without you having to work for it, you might still think you can get everything today just as easily, even when you can't afford it. As you might already know, having this kind of thinking can get you into big trouble in the future and bury you alive in a financial grave. If you didn't know this kind of thinking is dangerous, hopefully you will realize it after reading this book and hopefully prevent financial ruin.

Those of you who currently have no knowledge about how to manage your money (and/or do not have a "Napkin on the Fridge") more than likely often end up spending more than what you have.

Let's look again at those celebrities and athletes that make tons of money. Yes we're always hearing about how much they make per film, per game, per season etc., yet it seems like every other day we see in the news that one or another is in financial disarray, or completely broke! There are a variety reasons why this can happen. One of the main reasons is probably that the wrong principals and financial understanding were instilled in them when they were growing up. Some people just cannot handle the pressures of keeping up with those Joneses so they just spend, spend, spend. Some people act as though they have no limits when they are given credit or cash in their hands. They overdo it and break the bank.

Keep this phrase in mind when considering purchasing some of your "wants."

It's not how much money you make that is important, it's how much you keep.

It's all about the Green, right? Not the Red.

Money can be a valuable tool to achieve your dreams when you use it wisely.

Floyd Frumpy has often been heard saying things

like, "Make it Rain," "I'm Fab Floyd! I got Moneys, Honeys, and Cars that fly…I'm the Champ."

What a big difference between Uncle Floyd and his brother Fred. They are biological brothers with the same parents and upbringing, but when you look at the way they treat money; you'd definitely think Floyd was raised by royalty.

Uncle Floyd makes a fortune every time he fights or puts his name on a product or is seen in a commercial or TV program.

Fred is the owner of FrumpySOFT and makes his living, selling his software.

Both have lots of money and are very successful, so what is the difference?

The difference is, Fred understands the value of the money and how hard it is to make it and how easy it can be lost. It has taken many years of dedication and hard work to build his business and he made many mistakes along the way. Fred was forced to learn the value of money, because those mistakes showed him the importance of protecting his assets and how to plan for the future when his health could change for the worse.

Uncle Floyd on the other hand, thinks planning is a worry he can delay as long as he is fighting and raking in the money.

The value of the money for Fred is to enjoy and preserve for the future, while the value of money for Uncle Floyd is to enjoy today and worry about tomorrow only when a problem presents itself. He loves spending money on toys and ladies, let's not forget to mention how much he loves to "make it rain" dollar, dollar bills!

Uncle Floyd does not understand that the future is unpredictable and he can't fight forever. He has never stopped to ask what his plan is after he can't fight anymore or what would happen if he became seriously ill.

SAVE

Spend

Chapter XI

Financial Needs

To understand your own financial needs you need to know what your financial situation is and be able and answer the following key questions:

How much money do I need for short term goals such as emergency funds, rent, food, clothing, insurance, etc.?

How much money do I need for long term goals such as retirement or a house?

How much should I save every month/year?

How often should I review my financial goals?

Start with your "Napkin on the Fridge." Anything you might encounter in regards to your financial needs can be evaluated with the help of your budget. Be sure that it is always up to date and is simple enough for you to clearly see what's most important to your everyday living. Do this and it will be a great tool to help you plan your financial goals and figure out how to deal with a situation that may arise among other things you may have to deal with.

Let's check in with the Frumpys. Just the other day Auntie Frida was talking to a friend about her financial needs. She said her financial needs have changed since she and Flea got divorced. She is now more careful with her money and her spending habits.

Once she finally took the time to complete her "Napkin on the Fridge," it was like she was a new person. Of course, Frida still loves to spend money but she now has a purpose for each dollar she spends.

She is even planning to go on a cruise of a lifetime to Alaska, and is hoping to meet one of those surfers or just a nice single man that shares the same values in life she now enjoys. Since she is in the GREEN every month, it won't be long before she can book her ticket.

Chapter XII

Rent vs. Own

You may have already heard many theories about renting vs. buying a house and which is better. There really is not an exact science as to which is right, it all depends on your personal situation. You are the person who best knows and understands your budget, goals and dreams for the future.

For many people, purchasing a house is the ultimate "American Dream," even though this dream can cost your entire life savings.

It ultimately comes down to what your personal and financial goals are. For example, if you are at the beginning of your career and do not know where you are going to be in the next couple of years because you may move or travel as your job requires, it may be more wise to rent until you settle down.

Or maybe a mortgage doesn't fit in your budget just yet, and you need to share the rent with a buddy, so why not rent! It is all part of your I-plan.

What is a Mortgage?

"The charging of real (or personal) property by a debtor to a creditor as security for a debt (esp. one incurred by the purchase of the property), on the condition that it shall be returned on payment of the debt within a certain period time."

That is the exact definition, and for purposes of our discussion, it means you do not have enough cash to buy a house now, so you borrow the money from someone or a lending institution (typically a bank) and agree to pay back that amount (the debt) in periodic payments (usually monthly) over given a period of time (normally with interest). The reality is that until that mortgage is paid in full you actually own the debt, not the home. The lender, (the person/place you borrowed the money from) owns the home or property until the debt is paid off in full.

Imagine buying a house for $100,000 and agreeing to pay back the bank for it in full over the next 30 years. You did this because you don't have $100,000 in cash to buy it now outright. So instead you applied for credit in the amount of $100,000 loaned from the bank. The bank will first want to see your "Napkin on the Fridge" so make sure you bring it along with you if you are applying for credit with the bank. After the bank reviews your budget and sees that you are in the GREEN, you will have a good chance of obtaining credit from the bank to purchase that $100,000 home. However, you can be assured they will consider many additional factors before issuing you any credit.

So let's say they positively evaluated your "Napkin on the Fridge" AND the house was in good condition AND was worth the full $100,000 AND you were able to prove that you could pay back the full amount of the credit over next 30 years. Then you would likely be able to obtain the credit of $100,000 from the bank. During those next 30 years your debt will be $ 100,000 until you pay it in full.

So if you default, which is the term used for failure to make your payments, what do you think is going to happen? You got it, some big burly looking dudes are going to come knocking on the door to kick you out. So it is very important to think wisely about this major purchase, which is for most people, the largest purchase they'll ever make in life. However, if you plan ahead and set a goal you will be able to save enough to put a large down payment on a property. Keep in mind you must make sure you check your budget to see if you can afford to buy and maintain a home. Purchasing a home is an excellent way to build up your equity.

What is Equity?

There are a few meanings to what equity is exactly, however in terms of your I-plan, the best definition is "the residual value of a business or property beyond any mortgage thereon and liability therein."

To put it more simply, equity is equal to your total assets minus your liabilities.

Assets – Liabilities = Equity

So as you begin to think about when the right time to buy a home might be, take your time and crunch your numbers carefully, there are even lots of online calculators you can use to facilitate your decision making process as you evaluate all of your numbers. Take a few minutes and do an online search using the terms "rent vs. own calculator."

Another way to analyze whether you should buy or rent, according to one expert in financial planning is:

Look at the cross-over point. The cross-over point is about 15 times the annual cost of rent. In other words, as a rough rule of thumb, homes are probably fairly valued in a city when they cost about 15 times a year's rent. So, for example, if you're paying $10,000 a year to rent a place, think twice about buying a home that costs more than $150,000. Fifteen times is the historic average.

Remember it is all about your own situation and your own dreams and hopes for the future, so if purchasing a home fits on your "Napkin on the Fridge," and you have calculated all of your numbers and analyzed them thoroughly, go with what your gut tells you. Just make sure you feel confident about what you are purchasing or buying. Of course, there will always be those people who will question you, even your own mind will more than likely keep you up a few nights as you decide. But that's okay, this is a big decision and it should be looked at from all perspectives. However, at the end of the day the only one who will really know would be you and of course your "Napkin on the Fridge."

Fran asked her dad Fred for some advice to help her figure out if she should rent or buy a house. That's when Granny Frumpy said Fran should definitely buy a house. However, Fred told his mom that times have changed. He said it all depends on where you live and how the housing market is in that area, and of course whether she is stable enough in her job that she will be planning to live there for at least 7 years, would also be a factor.

Fran is planning to move into the new house or rental with her baby Fonzie. Fran will analyze all of the numbers on her "Napkin on the Fridge" and her work situation to see if it makes sense to buy. She knows that after looking at many homes she will need to apply for a mortgage at her local bank.

She also knows she will have to borrow the money from someone for her down payment. She is thinking her dad, Fred, might help her or if not she will have to save enough money on her own. Fred thinks if she buys a house, she should do it on her own in order to understand the responsibility that comes along with it. The first step is having enough savings.

After doing her homework, Fran now sees what her dad was saying because all of the banks she looked into required a 10-20% down payment, or more, in order to apply for a loan.

She found a really nice house that she likes, and knows Fonzie will be very excited to have his own house and own yard to run around in. Fonzie is her little baby, the cutest Pug you've ever seen!

Green Nugget: It is a good idea to only consider buying a house if you plan to live in it 7 years or more, especially if looking to get a mortgage from the bank or any lending institution. Most mortgage payments during the first few years of a loan are normally paid toward interest and not the principal owed. So make sure you ask for an amortization table from the lending institution before signing on the dotted line. The amortization table will show you year by year how much of your payment is paid toward interest and how much toward principal over the course of the loan. This is why Fred Frumpy stressed planning to live there for 7 years or more.

Chapter XIII

Buying or Leasing a Car

The question here is not should I take the bus or buy a car. The question is should I buy or lease a car?

When we bought the first car for my wife, it was a brand new Toyota. It was a sweet, limited edition model in a shiny silver. We decided to lease it for five years with the option to buy. We put a good amount down as required by the lease agreement and then we were able to drive the beautiful truck without any mechanical problems for five years. When the time came for us to buy or turn it in, we opted to turn it in. Why? Because of the cost to buy it would be 40% more than the fair market value (a fair price). Not a very good deal huh?

After that, it took us more than a year to get another car. We thought we could manage having only one car, and actually we did for more than 16 months. Of course there were times where I had my plans and she had hers. I took many rides from my buddies. And she would walk and bike as much as she could till the day we decided it was time to get another car.

This time around we did a lot of online searching and research and crunched our numbers carefully. We decided to buy a used car that was in great condition and we financed it. We thought that after 5 years the car could still hold some value. Or maybe it would be in good enough shape where we didn't need to buy a new car and it would be paid in full. We thought, why not? The key is to keep it in good condition and keep up with proper care, because if it is in good condition with no problems, it's even nicer when you have no payments and can cross that item off your "Napkin on the Fridge." And an item crossed off your "Napkin" equals GREEN CASH at the end of every month! So now maybe I can buy that watch I have always wanted.

When trying to decide which option is best for you, consider the following:

If you are a business owner, leasing might be a good idea, since you can generally deduct most of the lease payments being made if the vehicle is being used 100% for business purposes. When purchasing, there are substantial limitations placed by the tax code on how much of your vehicle can be deducted each year.

Do you want to have a new car every two or three years without having to make any major repairs? Then you should lease it.

Can you drive in a range determined by the agreement? Lease it.

Can you afford higher monthly payments and want to drive as many miles as you want? Buy it.

Do you care about building some equity? Buy it.

Do you like the idea of paying off your loan and being payment-free for a while? Buy it.

Do you like to customize your cars? Buy it.

The long-term cost of leasing is always more costly than buying, assuming the buyer keeps his or her vehicle after the loan is paid off.

Green Nugget: Cars are NOT a good investment. If you are purchasing a car with a car loan (otherwise known as financing), keep in mind like purchasing a home with a mortgage, the majority of the initial payments will be calculated towards paying the interest on the loan first. This is a hidden fact that sometimes will not be disclosed to you or seen, unless you ask for an amortization table from the lending institution or learn the hard way and sell your car within the first couple of years of the loan.

Let's check in again with the Frumpys.

Frank recently told Grandpa Frumpy that he wants to buy a new and reliable car. Frank says he is tired of having to take a bus or drive his clunker, which is always breaking down or in the shop being fixed.

Frank knows that he can't afford high payments and another problem is that his car insurance will be very high because of his age.

What do you think will be a good choice for him? Buy or lease? Or he could just keep riding the bus or driving the "junk box" for now.

Chapter XIV

College Planning

"College...gotta go to college, gotta get an education, gotta graduate from college...gotta...gotta...gotta, you can't be anyone in life if you don't get a college education."

Gotta is a whole-lotta nonsense when it comes to a college education. It's about time we take a serious look at what it means to go to college and obtain a higher education.

If you are planning to go to college at some point in your life, I would suggest you think about what it is that you really love to do.

Do you love to help people?

Do you love to play with numbers?

Do you love animals?

Do you love cars?

Do you love science?

Do you love to cook?

You GOTTA find your passion first. For many young folks, when the time comes to go to college and make the difficult decision of "what should I be when I grow up?" How many of us were lost? How many of us still are? Often times you are too young to know and you have no clue about your future.

My father was a professor and a big believer in higher education, it was basically mandatory in my household to go to college; not going was not even an option, at least that's the way I felt. I am sure many of you feel this way now or were made to believe the same way.

However, in this day and age, it is time we shift this mentality and start to see college for what it really is; it's a big business these days. It costs a lot of money to go to college and unlike years ago when you were almost 100% assured you were going to find a job after college in the area or field you studied, it is much less likely today. Times are different, and it's best we start having this discussion now. This is the root of many problems, and it is also why this chapter is so important.

College was meant to be for obtaining higher learning that can put you on the path to find an area of specialty so that you could make a living and ensure a prosperous future. It was not meant to be a Green Machine, taking in astronomical amounts of tuition, and spitting out kids with no direction or sense of accomplishment or passion for a specific field of study.

Think about how many young people go to college with the feeling that if their parents were or are teachers, then they should become one too. The same goes for those who have parents who were or are doctors, lawyers, business owners...etc. That is a lot of pressure.

The clock is ticking away, and you gotta go to college! Everyone has to go to college! Right? Well, Well, I want to know who made up this rule or law, parents it's time to tune in.

Maybe, you should take your time instead. Go and do some work during the summer months during high school, in an area you've always had an interest in. Talk to people and interview professionals in the area you feel you can actually see yourself working in the future. If you love cars, ask your local car shop if you could work as an intern for FREE at their shop. If you love science go to your local lab, hospital or research center and let them know you are willing to do anything they may need from you. If you love numbers or running a business, go to your local financial company and let them know you will print papers or do research for them. If you love building or construction, find a local construction company and let them know, you want to work for the summer for FREE or maybe minimum wage.

So you see, while you are in high school, and you have those summer months to enjoy and do whatever you wish, start thinking about your dreams and aspirations. What is it you want to be when you grow up? Reality is you probably will have no clue or just you think you do. Being willing to work for free as an intern will help you gain the knowledge about a particular industry that you always loved or were interested in. By the end of the summer, you should know if you loved it or you didn't or maybe it just wasn't what you expected. And that's okay, that's the best part, you are young and dumb. Like the song says "Time...is on my side...Yes it is!"

Please don't take me literally when I say "young and dumb," you are NOT dumb, you are actually just inexperienced at that age, but it would be wise to try things yourself and figure out if you're good at the things you enjoy before entering college. That's right...before entering college.

College is well-known for being some of the best years of your life. However, many of you that are parents now might think back to your college days and you may not even remember them, if you know what I mean. So take a step back from putting all that emphasis and pressure on your kids to go to college right out of high school. You don't want to end up putting your retirement assets at stake to send your kids to college, just because that's what kids were "supposed" to do back in the day. Times are different now and we have to start teaching our young larvae, that in order to become a butterfly, it will take years of experience and learning.

Next we'll talk about how we can change the game. Oh my professors are going to love me for this one. After reading this, you can probably expect to see me on the news getting either loving or hateful comments from all my favorite professors, or perhaps even getting kicked off college campuses. This might be because of my theory that many young people are not ready for college and that Green Machine (the institutions of higher learning) sure don't want all of those young people to agree with that.

How about we turn the table, and say college is not ready for YOU. That's right; you have to figure out why you want to go to college and what it is you want to get out of college? Remember, going to college is a very big expense. So if you are planning to go to college and party like a rock star and end up graduating, still not having a clue of which direction you want to take your life, then college is NOT ready for YOU! You know that college fund mom and dad saved for you? Guess what, it's now turned into a loan that you will be required to pay back.

That's right; it's time for parents to wake up! It's time we let our children, who will be the future of our country, know that there is NO free lunch in this world, so why have we been teaching them that for so long?

And for all my young rock stars, join a band and show your talents at the local night club to see if anyone is willing to pay to see you perform. If you don't make it in the music world, you'll know college or maybe the military may make more sense for you. Yes, that's right, the military. By joining the military you can learn a trade or a skill and many times the military will even cover your college tuition after serving with them. The military can also help you grow-up, learn manners and become a professional and respected adult (parents love to hear that). Your time spent in the military can also help you figure out what you are good at or what you enjoy doing.

At some point you will figure out what you want to do with your life, that's the good news. However, the bad news might be that you spend four years or more going to college and come out still not knowing what you want to do.

Just remember to never simply accept your parent's desires for your future as your own. They are your parents' dreams, and they may not be your dreams now or in the future.

You only have one life and once you get in the "Real World," you will want to enjoy work and be passionate about what you do, including all of the "work and hustle" that comes along with it.

I have heard so many people complaining about their jobs and salaries. They live a miserable life. And many are the same people that have master's degrees or higher and graduated from the best colleges in the country. Often times it's those people who never figured out what their true passion was and now they are stuck with a lot of debt, remember that earlier chapter on debt? Just to recap, you own the debt (or maybe your parents own it) either way, it is just NOT cool.

You do not want to invest your time and money in something you can't use or that won't end up making you more money in the end. Today, colleges and universities have become GREEN money machines. They charge high tuition fees, books, and living expenses. I have yet to find a college that advertises or says, "If you don't have a job in the industry of your choice after graduating, we will refund your entire tuition."

So, why is that?

Don't get me wrong. Knowledge is very powerful. Being educated is powerful too, and getting degree in the field of your choice is also very important. But you should not have to break your piggy bank or rob your parents' nest egg to accomplish finding out what it is you have a passion for, what are you good at, what your talents are, what can you do that is different than others or what makes you special.

Your passion will make you successful. Your drive and desire to succeed, no matter how high the mountain might be to climb, will help you get to the top. Remember it is your mountain to climb, no one else's. You can be anything you want to be, sounds good, right? Well it is true. In sports, we call it the "Will to Win."

If you have the will power and the work ethic and the belief in yourself, you can and will achieve whatever it is that your heart and mind desire.

I have met many business owners and successful people that did not need a master's degree or a degree from one of the best colleges in order to become successful.

Unless you love titles and abbreviations after your name, then that is a whole other story. We can all pass tests. That's right all of us! We may have to study harder and longer than others, but the reality is that you can do anything you put your mind to, if you want to do it bad enough, YES YOU CAN. I can say this because I am probably the worst test taker there is, but have passed over 25 hours of examinations for my business. If I can do it, I know you can too. So first take the time necessary to learn what it is you really want to do with your life, because that's the hard part. The easy part is figuring out how to pass the many tests and examinations that will most likely be required. But hey, isn't life a test, every day we wake? And you get through it, right?

Like I said, no matter which major you choose or career path you desire, the only thing you gotta have is passion and the love for what you are doing.

This is why I am not a big fan of parents messing with their retirement or postponing their retirement plan as a way to fund a college education for their kids. If a young person really needs the money, they can always get a loan or work hard to earn a scholarship. Like the value of money, the same can be applied here for education.

Do your research before you get a student loan, just as you would for any other type of loan. Most importantly, make sure you are on the same page as your parents as far as your purpose for going to college and what you want to get out of going to college.

Do not pay unnecessary high costs for college. With online degree programs, tech schools, community colleges, military, and so many other places available to us for free, there is no reason for paying ridiculously high prices for the same degree. Do your research and compare different schools.

Go out and make it happen. Remember, all you need is will power! Good things will be waiting for you.

And, for those of you who might have read this chapter and said, "I am not working for FREE," here is another little

Green Nugget: That FREE work you could go out and get, will someday really help you put money in your pocket. You will know what I mean after you try it. My suggestion is to try it while you are in high school, and if you are already in college or beyond and are still trying to figure out what makes you happy, try it! Then you can turn around and later tell those naysayers how that "Free Work" or minimum wage job put more Green on your "Napkin on the Fridge," than you could ever imagine it would have.

Just keep in mind that it may take years before you will understand what I have been saying, for now just believe in YOU.

Let's check back in with the Frumpy Family, I am sure they've had to deal with this. Fred and Flo always talked about the future of their kids and what would be best for them in the future.

Would they want to follow in Fred's footsteps and become part of his software business? Would they want to pursue another career?

Fred and Flo agreed that they would let their kids decide their future careers on their own. Of course, their parents would help guide them along and be supportive in helping them find their passion in life.

Their daughter Fran graduated with a degree in Business Administration from a reputable online university. She is taking extra courses in finance to stay up to date in her career at her dad's company FrumpySoft, where she works in the financial department.

The Frumpy's son Frank still does not know what he wants to do. So he decided to wait one more year before applying to any college. He is even thinking about going to culinary school instead of a traditional college because he absolutely loves to cook. In the meantime, Frank is working with Granny Frumpy at her real estate company. He helps her with the management and maintenance of all the properties she owns.

Both Fran and Frank worked at the local ice cream parlor and even delivered pizza while they were in high school. These jobs helped them realize the value of money and how difficult it was to earn a paycheck, and how much extra work it took to earn a big paycheck.

Frank is still amazed about how Uncle Floyd is always able to "make it rain." He is always dreaming about what it would be like to live that way, but he knows he does not have the passion or talent that Floyd did for a sport.

Fred Frumpy always says, "Passion for what you do will always be the secret to your success."

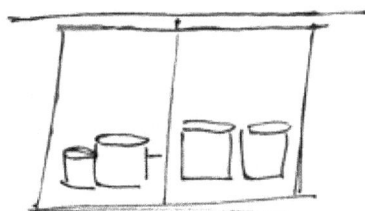

Chapter XV

The Basics of Insurance

Insurance means protection. Protection against the unexpected.

Do you need insurance?

Many people only buy insurance when it is mandatory by law or the bank. Many people do this because they do not believe in insurance and they think insurance is a waste of money.

Let me tell you, I know many stories about people that lost everything because they did not have insurance. And they regret not purchasing insurance after something terrible happened, in other words, when it was too late.

I will always remember the story about a friend of mine. Her husband canceled his life insurance policy eight months before he died of a heart attack. His wife tried to fight the insurance company, but unfortunately it was too late. I thought my friend's husband was totally crazy to cancel a policy knowing his health condition.

Once you stop paying the premiums (the monthly payments to the insurance company) you are truly living on the edge with the chance you could lose it all. And I mean this about everything: your car, your house, your life, your health, your assets, your business, etc.

So take a few minutes to think about all that you have been working hard to achieve as well as all the things you want to purchase for yourself and your family. If you are not protected, a simple accident can put you in a big financial hole that can cause stress you wouldn't believe.

Insurance is there to protect yourself and your assets. Remember: Life is full of risks and hope is not a plan.

You cannot drive without car insurance.

Your health is your true wealth, so make sure you protect it with health insurance.

Your home may be your biggest asset, so why wouldn't you want it protected if something were to happen due to weather, fire, accident, or even as simple as someone slipping and falling on your sidewalk and you being sued because of negligence or something that you had no control over.

The point is always protect yourself, and use insurance to your advantage.

Green Nugget: Insurance costs change from year to year, each company is always competing for your business to increase their revenues and profitability. This is good news for you. You should consider carefully shopping around for your car insurance, homeowners insurance coverage and even your health insurance coverage if you are not on a company plan. This can be a time consuming process, but there are professional insurance brokers that can do this for you, and online quote systems that can assist you. Just make sure to compare plans apples to apples, read the policy coverage sheet and make a few calls directly to some of the more highly rated companies in your state, as each state will differ. This is a well-kept secret, so don't be lazy or complacent with the coverage you have, especially if you have a good record of not making many claims or been with a carrier for a certain amount of years with no negative marks on your record.

Do this exercise yearly on your anniversary. Make the call today, and if I am able to save you more than the cost of this book, spread the good word to a friend, family member, or just a stranger, they too can have a healthier pocket with an I-Plan.

Chapter XVI

Understanding Life Insurance

Let's start by learning and understanding the importance of having life insurance. You are going to live a long and healthy life, right? But you do not have enough time to research and purchase a life insurance plan. Think about it though, you could get sick and die at any moment. "Wow!" you might be thinking, "Did he just say that? Is he kidding?" Unfortunately I am not.

Take it from me, my father was Ph.D. in Physical Education and Recreation, the guy just loved sports. He played and coached at the highest levels, and just like that after he played a tennis match, at the age of 49 that was it. They do say the good die young. Yep, even that young, it could be you today or tomorrow, sad to say like Frank Sinatra would say, "That's Life," if you don't know who Frank Sinatra is...oh boy, no worries, time...really is on your side. You will learn, life really does go on, but to have a plan in place gives you a feeling of peace of mind and a comfort knowing your family will never have to struggle.

Fortunately for my family, my father had a life insurance plan in place that allowed us to continue pursuing our dreams and for my mom to be able to continue living the same lifestyle as she had been living. This was all possible because of the proceeds from his life insurance policy he had planned and paid for monthly.

That's why there is life insurance; to make sure your loved ones will be in a safe place and secure an income for them when you may not be by their side anymore.

Still there are so many people that insure their cars, homes and other things that are replaceable, but they don't insure themselves, which are NOT replaceable.

Don't you think a life lived with peace of mind is worth a few hundred bucks a year?

If you do, let's get to know more about the types of life insurance plans that are out there. I promise I will give you a short and clear explanation, so that you don't get confused like your mind often might when dealing with complicated matters like life insurance. I don't want you to be able to go another day saying, "I will address it tomorrow it's too confusing."

Don't let your mind play tricks on you so that you just keep putting it off and it ends up hurting those you care about most. Life is precious, I think everyone would agree. So don't let human nature allow you to procrastinate in taking action against the most precious thing you have, LIFE.

Term Insurance: Term insurance is generally relatively cheap in price, especially if you don't have many assets or emergency reserves, but you do have financial dependents. There is no cash build-up with these policies.

Think of term insurance like renting. A fixed payment for a certain period of time, after that period-term is up so is your insurance with zero equity/cash.

If the insured dies during the term, the death benefit will be paid to the beneficiary. Term insurance is the least expensive way to purchase a substantial death benefit for a certain amount of coverage per premium dollar basis over a specific period of time.

Whole Life Insurance: It gives you lifelong protection. Your premiums at the beginning are higher to help cover the costs of providing you that protection later in life when term insurance premiums get costly. It has a savings component that earns cash value. Think of whole life insurance like buying a house. A mortgage payment for a certain period of time, after a certain period of time you own the policy with equity/cash and no more payments and you own the insurance for life.

And next is my favorite option for all my young, financially savvy readers.

Variable Life Insurance: It is the same as whole life insurance, but will give you the ability to have much of your cash that is in the policy invested in various types of investments. Consider this policy when you are young, your cost of insurance will be cheap, and allow most of your premiums to be invested so later on the cash you accumulate can be used someday for another discussion.

Universal Life Insurance: This is a flexible payment option policy. This type of life insurance policy will earn you interest amounts depending on the cash value of the initial policy and how the company you select performs. The interest credited to your policy from the insurance company will fluctuate, usually yearly. You are also able to withdraw, borrow from the policy or utilize interest credits/dividends to be applied to your premium to reduce your premium, as long as your payments are up to date.

Survivorship Life Insurance: This type of insurance helps you to protect your wealth from Uncle Sam. This is a policy that will pay a death benefit upon two individual's deaths. This is for more advanced planning later in life.

There are many life insurance strategies that can be applied to different situations. So it is always a good idea to talk to a financial adviser that specializes in or has extensive knowledge when it comes to life insurance. Or talk to an insurance professional who understands the various options available and the best approach for you and your family.

Just make sure you talk to someone who believes in life

insurance. There are many professionals that I have run across that somehow think anyone is better off without insurance, ask them do they have insurance? If so, why? If not, why not? If they say they don't have life insurance, think twice about their recommendations.

Green Nugget: Ask yourself, how can you take advice from someone giving advice who does not believe in their advice enough to take it for themselves?

Insurance, while it may seem confusing, is actually a simple concept, and a very powerful financial planning tool. In fact, it might be the most powerful financial planning tool we have available to us, from a tax planning standpoint. You should think of insurance as a gift to the ones we cherish the most. Someone very successful once said, "I will always spend pennies to protect dollars." Now that's a green nugget for your I-Plan.

Life insurance is important to protect the ones that we love and still many people do not insure themselves. This is why there are so many people that are left behind in financial hardship each year. Their spouse or loved one dies without having some type of protection and the family now is left struggling to take care of the expenses and everyday bills that are, unfortunately, a part of living.

As your pocket gets healthier and healthier over time, you will begin to learn that insurance also plays a much more powerful role in your strategic financial planning. You should speak with an expert or qualified adviser who understands life insurance so that they can explain further, and not one who is just trying to sell you insurance (use that insurance person to compare pricing if need be). Always ask for an illustration showing you the guarantees in your policy and the non-guarantees, and read the fine print to make sure you know what you are buying, or have your questions and concerns answered by your insurance professional.

Green Nugget: Those who started a life insurance policy that builds cash at a young age, are able to take advantage of their great health which means they will have low cost of insurance premiums, and over time will build Cash...Moolah. There are many wise "Yodas" that will tell you that they bought their dream retirement cottage, funded their kids educations and didn't even pay premiums later in life, all thanks to the various types of life insurance vehicles. So for those who might say insurance is a waste of money, you now have a little green nugget to consider when evaluating your life insurance options for your "healthy pocket" straight from our wise Jedi Knights.

Green Nugget: By having life insurance, it gives you the right to spend what you earn.

The telephone is ringing at Granny Frumpy's house. It's her daughter-in-law Flo and she's crying. It isn't long before Granny starts to cry too.

What happened?

Fred Frumpy suffered a heart attack and passed away that morning while getting ready for work. He was just 48 years old.

Life is like a feather, it is so delicate.

Flo quit working a long time ago and now she has Frank (20 years old) and Fran (29 years old) to help support her through this hard time.

Flo now will be the sole owner of FrumpySoft. Do you think Fred had a plan in case the worse happened as it just has?

From what Flo knows, Fred bought life insurance a long time ago. Fred was a business owner and wanted to make sure his loved ones would be ok if something bad like this ever happened.

Fortunately, Fred purchased life insurance years ago with the financial advice from his trusted advisers, knowing it would be the only insurance he would someday collect on, 100%.

He knew with the right policy and estate and business plan in place, Flo and his kids would never have to worry, life would go on and their finances were protected.

Chapter XVII

Understanding Disability Insurance

We have talked about life insurance, which is important in case you die. Now we'll talk about another bad situation. What if you become disabled and unable to work for an uncertain period of time?

This would be pretty bad news, however the good news is that there is insurance you can purchase to protect yourself and your income if something like this were to happen. This type of insurance is called disability insurance; it's very affordable and should be looked at as a must if you are working. Why? Think about it, if you became disabled and couldn't work, where would your income come from?

Disability Insurance: This insurance replaces a portion of your income in the event you become disabled and are no longer able to work. Just like life insurance, prices will vary based on a variety of factors including one's age, gender, profession, the amount of coverage, and health status. Believe it or not, it's very inexpensive.

Many people think that disabilities are typically caused by freak accidents, but the majority of long term absences from work are actually due to sudden illnesses, such as cancer and heart disease. The loss of income during this time can be so devastating that it forces many people to foreclose on their homes, lose their entire life savings, or even declare bankruptcy.

Always think about how you would financially support your family in case of the unexpected, especially knowing the likelihood of suffering a long term disability is 1 in every 3 people at some point in life. That's not the best of odds, is it?

Remember building a "healthy pocket" is just as important as making sure it's protected. No one wants to be pick-pocketed. Now that it is easy to see, now that you are armed with this information, there is no reason your pocket will ever be in danger.

I suggest that you start to think of insurance as a fixed expense. This way you can make sure that it's on that side of your "Napkin on the Fridge." You need to start thinking of it as a need and not a want.

You may not qualify for life insurance or disability insurance, but that does NOT mean you don't have options. What it really means is that you need to take that money you were planning to pay for premiums with, and make sure you put it to good use for your protection. Work with someone who can talk to you about the various options based on your situation. Just remember that if you don't qualify for insurance it often means you are a RISK to the insurance company, which should mean to you, don't RISK putting this subject off for your family, and put a plan in place TODAY!

Another Green Nugget: Many people who work for a medium to large company will normally have life insurance and disability insurance offered through the company with no health requirements; you just have to pay the monthly premium with no questions asked. If you are not in good health, it's even more important that you always sign up for this benefit. If you are in excellent health it is often much cheaper (pending your age/profession/state of health) to purchase it on your own. Understand that "group insurance" is, on average, more expensive than individual insurance, if you are in good health. So be sure that you compare the two, but if you can't get insurance on your own, whatever the amount offered to you at work is, take it and ask for the maximum amounts available. It will be deducted from your paycheck.

The Frumpys know all about the benefits of insurance. Recently, Uncle Floyd noticed Flea had been acting very weird for the last few days. Uncle Floyd noticed something bad was going on with Flea. "Maybe he is upset because Auntie Frida has a new boyfriend," Uncle Floyd thought.

Uncle Floyd is about to find out just what was wrong. Recently, Flea had begun calling doctors and clinics, which is very unusual for him because he is the one that always avoids doctors.

One day Uncle Floyd saw lots of different exam reports on Flea's desk. To make matters worse, he also heard Flea on the phone with someone talking about what sounded like cancer. Could it really be?

"Cancer? NO! Not Flea," Uncle Floyd thought, "he's one of the strongest guys you'll ever meet physically, emotionally, and mentally." Flea was Uncle Floyd's rock.

Another time that Flea was on the phone, Uncle Floyd overheard him speaking with his financial advisor about the disability insurance he purchased a few years ago, just in case one day he would be unable to manage and train Floyd anymore.

Flea was asking his advisor if his disability policy would cover cancer, and if he would be able to collect the same income he is currently receiving while working for Uncle Floyd, should he not be able to work anymore.

The good news, is that Flea is in fact protected

and his insurance policy will replace his income while he is undergoing treatment. The toughest part maybe knowing Uncle Floyd's rock, Flea may never again be in his corner. Uncle Floyd just lost his brother and now might lose his best friend during the biggest moments of their careers.

Chapter XVIII

When to Begin Investing
** Invest in yourself**

In this chapter we are going to talk about YOU.

There are a lot of demands placed on you every day. These demands can come from your partner, your boss, your family, even your bestest buddy (your pet) demands some attention from you.

Sometimes you may feel so overwhelmed by all the pressure that you feel as though you just are not going to make it to the finish line. You might feel like all of your energy is gone with the wind. But don't worry, you are not alone. Just talk to a few people and you'll see that a lot of other people have the same feelings.

So what if you just can't do it anymore? What is going to happen to you? What will happen to your future? What will happen to those that you love the most?

Stop for a moment and be selfish. Put yourself first. Put your goals, your dreams, most importantly your health first. We often forget our true wealth is our health. So take care of yourself, your mind and body. That's the only way you can then give value and take care of others.

And this theory applies for investments too. Invest in yourself or pay yourself first. To do this, you will need to save 10% of your gross income every month. We all know sometimes it is hard because of all those bills we have to pay, but...

Remember this Green Nugget: "You need money to make money." Say what?

It means you need to save up some money before you can start investing. First of all you should have your savings plan in place. Do your homework and look at "Napkin on the Fridge" often and try your hardest to put aside some cash every month. Remember it's your financial future that you are building here! It is YOU first!

Take your time to educate yourself about how to build your nest egg. Do your homework, do online research, read books and interview various professionals, financial advisors and planners, insurance professionals, accountants, bankers, and attorneys in that order. The more educated you are, the more you will be able to accomplish your financial goals. Just by reading this book you have taken a great step forward. Invest in yourself, and your education and you will see great rewards in return.

One last quick point to mention, remember that we are all different and have very different situations, just because your friend or family member says something or is doing something different than you, does not mean they are doing things right or would work for you. I often times hear, "my friend or family member said you should do this or that." So it's like the old saying, if they are planning to jump off the cliff, are you going to join them? This can also be said for financial advisors seen on TV or heard on the radio or the guy or gal writing a financial column in the newspaper, magazine, or especially a blog. Take those opinions for what they are worth, they may be so-called experts in their field or they might not be, just remember that there is only one real expert on your financial freedom team and that is going to be YOU, because you have an I-Plan.

Invest in yourself and work toward your financial freedom. It does not happen overnight. You have to work hard at it every day, and do it on your terms - no one else's.

Green Nugget: When the time is right for you to begin investing in whatever it may be, consider the following idea, which is one of the most important investment fundamentals that no investment guru can argue with when it comes to average folks like you and me.

Dollar Cost Averaging = Systematic investment into your account

This fundamental approach to investing, whether it is $25 a month, $1,000 a month or $10,000 a month, is the most important fundamental to always remember when investing. In short, it's all about consistency; stick to it!

Consider having your investment automatically deducted from your paycheck or bank account and invested on a day of the month you will have money available or feel lucky.

This proven philosophy will help you avoid trying to time the markets you are investing in and trying to buy low and sell high. The very best investors all over the world understand that no one can time the markets. Some self proclaimed "investing pros" might say they can, but we know better by now; no one can predict the future.

So use this green nugget on your journey toward financial success. Remember you must have something to start with, even if it is very small $25 a month. Over time you will be able to set aside more, but will have your systematic plan in place and be able to enjoy the highs and the lows of the market over time, especially remember to stick with the plan you have established because the markets will always go up and down. Also, always remember to re-evaluate your overall investment structure periodically with your advisor.

Disclosure: Dollar Cost Averaging and diversification does not protect against a loss in a declining market.

Chapter XIX

Risk Tolerance/Investment Objective/Time Horizon

Here we go! I will give you an idea on how to start investing. Who knows, you may become the next billionaire. Think about how that one certain billionaire started back in the day, maybe at just six years old. He purchased a bunch of 6-packs of Coca-Cola from his grandpa's grocery store for twenty five cents and resold each of the bottles for a nickel, pocketing a five cent profit, anyone know who that was?

Let's say you started out at seven years old selling lemonade and also made profit – but your mom made the lemonade for you, right? Or maybe you figured out selling lemonade didn't make very much money for you, or your location was bad. So instead you went door to door offering to cut grass or shovel snow. Or maybe you tried washing cars, selling candy in school, babysitting, house sitting or whatever it might be, just as long as you made sure what you were doing was completely legal. You know what I am talking about? Illegal actions will almost always come back to haunt you. Some will call it easy money, but you will learn the hard way like the rest of them, Al Capone, Bernie Madoff and Pablo Escobar, just to name a few; the list goes on and on. And if you don't know who they are, just turn on our evening news there is always someone who was living life in the fast lane only to be caught for easy money schemes involving theft, fraud, money-laundering, tax-evasion, drug dealing and lots of other illegal activities.

If there is anything you can learn from experience, is that you have to work long, hard hours to perfect yourself and what it is you are doing. Sometimes there is no immediate result, maybe no neighbors stopped to buy your lemonade the first day. It is ok, just be patient and work smarter not harder.

Green Nugget: Patience is a virtue.

Success in investing requires patience. You have to understand that you are going to invest for the long term. You are going to invest to win. You are going to invest to create wealth and protect it. All while doing it the right way, being honest with yourself and those you work with.

Some people choose to invest to reach a certain goal. For example: you want to invest in order to have enough money for college, or to buy a house, or to buy a car. Maybe it is time to think about your retirement.

Whatever your goal is, write it down. Always write down your goals, the more you see them, the sooner they will become reality.

Don't you want to be your own financial expert of your I-Plan? That is after all, what matters most, You and your plan, right? To do this you must always evaluate three, very important, fundamental financial principles.

The three most important questions you have to ask yourself before you make any investment have to do with:

Investment Objective, Time Horizon, Risk Tolerance

Investment Objective

What is the end goal, what is the purpose, the objective of your investment?

Time Horizon

What kind of timeline do you have before you need to use

your investment?

Ask yourself for how long will you need to invest towards your goal and how much money will you need?

You will have to get very familiar with your "Napkin on the Fridge" and know your numbers like the back of your hand and revise them from time to time in order to see how much you've accomplished or what adjustments you may need to make.

Risk Tolerance

How much financial risk can you take, or should we say how much you can afford to lose?

More risk often times means more reward, less risk often times means less reward.

With your goals in mind, let your age and current stage in life guide you when it comes to your risk tolerance.

The term financial risk means the ability to absorb the ups and downs you will have or see with your investment.

Investments may include things such as stocks, bonds, mutual funds, gold, real estate, options and commodities.

If you are in your 20s, 30s or 40s, you will be able to be more aggressive and put a larger percentage of your investments into riskier assets. You are still building your wealth so you have "time on your side."

Investing in your future means making some sacrifices in the present moment (today) in order to reach a goal for the future (tomorrow). I am sure you know many people that only think in terms of "today," spending their money on things that do not bring value for their "tomorrow."

To put it more simply, invest your time and money on things that may not give you immediate return, but which will give you more value or opportunities later on.

If you are in your 50s or older, or about to retire you should be more conservative and begin to think more towards the idea of wealth preservation (protecting your assets) and examining ways to provide for income for the rest of your years, when the time comes that you want to finally say, "I want to enjoy all the years of my labor, time to enjoy my glory years." At this time in your life you should be able to sleep very well at night with no financial worries. No babies crying anymore, no kids to support, no more stress at work, it's your glory years, to do as you please...all because of your I-Plan.

No matter how old you are, keep in mind that preparing the garden now is essential to enjoying its fruits later on.

Chapter XX

Investment Vehicles

To make things real simple, I will sort out each of the various investment vehicles by how risky they are.

Examples of low risk investments are those that provide a very low return on investment and little or no inflation protection and can be easily liquidated into cash.

Cash equivalents: Liquid money or emergency reserve money
Cash
Savings accounts
Certificates of deposit (CDs)

Money market funds
Here I want to point out that inflation protection means that as the cost of living goes up every year, so too will your money or investment.

Examples of low risk investments designed to protect against inflation:

Fixed income vehicles (ex. annuities)   Municipal bonds
Government bonds   High quality corporate
Bond funds   Treasury securities

Examples of moderate/growth/aggressive risk investments:

Stocks   Stock/bond mutual funds
Exchange traded funds   Moderate yield bonds
Real Estate Investment Trust (REIT)   Privately held Real
Estate

These can offer a balance between risky and long term quality return.

Examples of speculative risk investments:

Futures contracts   Stock options
High yield bonds (junk bonds)   Hedge funds
Precious metals and gems   Penny stocks (Microcap stocks)
Emerging markets   High risk mutual funds and
ETFs
Short selling
Antiques, stamps, coins and other collectibles
Foreign Exchange Market (currency, Forex or FX)

Before you begin investing, first make sure your emergency or "rainy day" fund has been established and is stable. Then you can begin evaluating your options with the help of a financial professional. I would encourage you to find an advisor that is a fiduciary. This way he or she can help you determine the right investment approach while making sure he or she takes into account your investment objective, time horizon, and risk tolerance.

A fiduciary advisor has a legal responsibility to put the client's needs ahead of their own interests.

A fiduciary advisor has a legal responsibility to put the client's needs ahead of their own interests.

"Age 100 Rule"

A simplistic approach to your overall investment plan is by using the "Age 100 Rule." Take your current age and subtract it from 100.

For example, we will use a 65 year old. So we take 100 and subtract their age, 65, so that 100 - 65 = 35. In terms of low risk money and moderate/growth/aggressive risk money, this person should now use 65 and 35 as their parameters. That means 35% of their retirement dollars should be allocated to some type of moderate/growth/aggressive oriented investment plan. The remaining 65%

should be in a plan that is little to low risk focusing on investments that are designed to prevent loss of principal. A key point to keep in mind is to always remember to make sure you add 10 if you are on a fixed income, this will help insure extra safety against any loss of principal.

This rule is not an exact science and should only be used to provide yourself with a gauge of how you should consider structuring your investments. It is most important to work with a professional, do your homework and take into account the three main fundamental you read about earlier: investment objective, time horizon and risk tolerance. You always want to make sure your investment approach matches these three fundamentals principles. Remember it's your money and investment not your parents', family member's, friend's or neighbor's and definitely not your attorney's, agent's, manager's, accountant's, planner's or your advisor's, it's YOUR MONEY, so be smart when it comes to asking questions and always do your own homework.

Never let the newspaper financial section, radio, TV analysts, or anyone else make you believe there is a one size that fits all approach to investing. If anything it's the opposite, no size fits all.

Everyone has an opinion, so take that opinion for what it's worth. Keep this in mind mostly, when listening to the guys and gals who tell you the investment markets are going up or down, whether it is just a little bit or a lot.

Green Nugget: Do you really think these people would be telling you the investment market secrets if they really knew what they were? Sure they may have educated insight from experience and research, but the reality is, NO ONE KNOWS WHERE THE MARKETS ARE GOING, SO JUST STICK TO THE FUNDAMENTALS THAT YOU HAVE LEARNED HERE!

You know what they say; slow and steady wins the race. So if you are looking for get rich quick schemes, good luck; just don't forget that as fast as the money might come, it can go just as fast, if not faster. Take a minute to look back on what we can learn from some examples in history. The dot-com bubble, POP! The housing bubble POP!! The credit bubble POP!!! What's next to pop? The gold bubble? Who knows? I can assure you those "experts" don't know, because if they did, do you really believe they would tell you their secrets, unless they had some kind of agenda? It is more logical to think that they would keep those secrets to themselves so that they could make the money, not you, or better yet tell you those so-called secrets so that they can make money off of you. Just think about it.

I don't want to name names, because that just isn't cool, but I am sure you have seen those crazy talkers on TV and on Radio, or those infomercials or internet ads that intimidate you into investing. My advice is just be $mart!

I always get leery of those that say "trust me" or someone who tries to instill fear in me to make a decision. I will usually run for the hills when I hear this and you should too. The best one is when I hear them say things like "my clients have never lost money" or "my clients make this or that percent every year." Yeah, sure! If it sounds too good to be true, make sure to ask a lot of questions, do your homework and never jump into something or feel pressured into making a decision you don't feel fully confident in. You always want to feel confident and comfortable about your investment and money and the people you are working with in making decisions about that money.

We have heard a lot of scams over the years, and we have seen a lot of these shysters, scam artists and EZ Money guys. It is easy to blame them for the financial situation of many Americans, but now it's time we blame ourselves.

We can learn from the past mistakes of others. These are just some basic lessons that are being laid out for you on a silver platter for you enjoy, so eat it up!

Here is a fundamental Green Nugget:
Think TWICE before you invest more than 5% of your portfolio in ONE company's stock. Important lessons have been learned from the history of the many companies that were once ICONS to no longer be in existence or on their way out of existence. These are lessons that should have finally been learned by now, especially from those that lost their entire life savings because of certain companies' lack of innovation or the crooked and greedy ways that were used at the top.

THINK TWICE BEFORE YOU EVER INVEST MORE THAN 5% in ONE COMPANY's STOCK, THIS IS NOT ADVISABLE TO MOST INVESTORS.

I am not sure how much clearer I can be, so if you choose otherwise, just remember that you were WARNED!

Let's check in with our friends the Frumpys.

Grandpa Frumpy is still driving his old Mercedes Benz. He is 70 years old and doesn't care about speed limits. He doesn't see all that well anymore so the lines don't mean much when he parks his car. He might be a little reckless when driving, but that's why he has a handicap tag; so no big deal, right? He has earned his privilege to drive.

What is more dangerous is how he takes risks with his investments at his age. He invests more than half of his money in two different companies' stocks and has always said that America would collapse if a certain auto company, telephone company, insurance company or bank were to collapse... hmm, can you think of a few that did collapse?

Some years ago, along with the rest of America, Grandpa Frumpy saw many of his stocks drop.

His financial advisor told Grandpa that at his advanced age he should not be taking that many risks, because he doesn't have the time left to wait and hope for them to rebound. His advisor suggested that Grandpa Frumpy should be thinking about how to protect his lifelong savings for himself as well as his family.

Grandpa Frumpy understands, but sometimes people get greedy and might trust their so-called "advisors" that say they can make fortunes. And by now you should have learned that in the financial world, what is too good to be true, usually is just that. There is a catch somewhere in the deal.

So how should Grandpa Frumpy invest at his age? Let's try the "Age 100 rule" you learned earlier for Grandpa Frumpy.

100-70= 30% in growth investments and 70% in protected income.

How about for Uncle Floyd? Uncle Floyd is 36 years old, so 36= 100-36= 64% in aggressive/growth investments and 36% in protected income.

However, knowing the way Uncle Floyd feels about money, he can probably be 100% aggressive, because for someone like Floyd, just knowing he actually has a diversified investment plan in place is a huge step in the right direction. But always remember that everyone is different.

How about Fran? Fran is 29, so 100-29 = 71% in more aggressive/growth investments and 29% in protected income.

How about auntie Frida? Frida is 45, so 100-45= 55% in aggressive/growth investments and 45% in protected income.

How about Fonzie (the Pug)? Fonzie is 4 years old, so 100-4= 100% in bones and dog food!

Remember these are just examples and are a good starting point to work with, but you will need to have your three principals in place before considering.
Investment Objective, Risk Tolerance, Time Horizon.

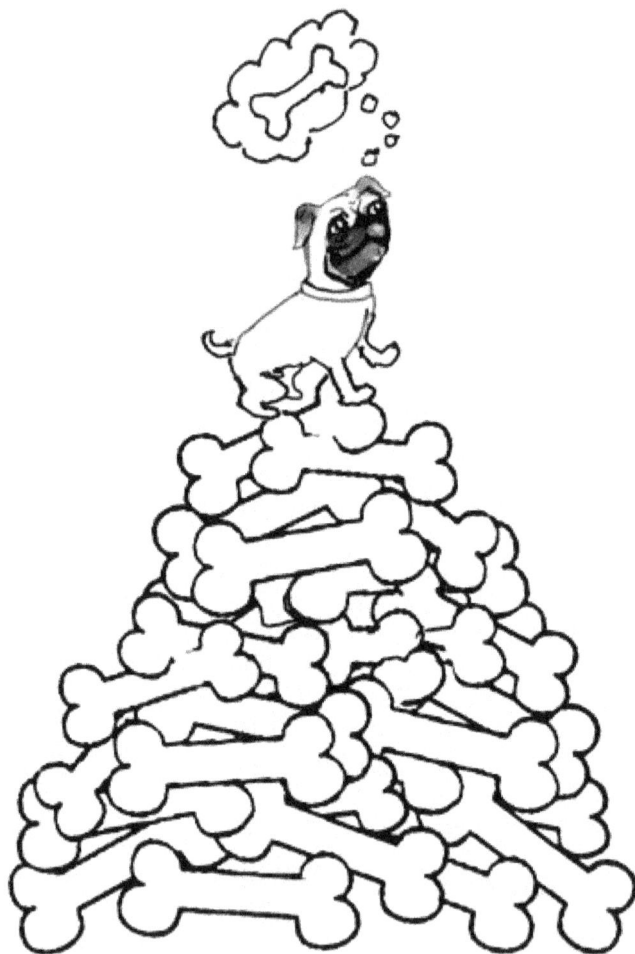

Chapter XXI

Retirement Vehicles

Time really does fly, and as we get older it is true that it only seems to be going by faster with each year that passes. So if you don't plan for your future, who will do it for you? Don't rely on the government, on your family or even that weekly lottery ticket. Let's be real, those thoughts are definitely not going to secure a comfortable retirement.

Before we move on, let me say that one more time...THE GOVERNMENT WILL NOT SOLVE OUR PROBLEMS, so STOP WITH THE POLITICAL SLOGANS and BELIEVING THEM.

It is time to step up and say "PEOPLE SOLVE PROBLEMS, WE THE PEOPLE! I WILL SOLVE MY PROBLEMS! NO ONE ELSE, NOT MY PARENTS, NOT CHILDREN, NOT GOVERNMENT, NO ONE WILL, BUT ME!"

I know for some, you may be thinking: I'm too young or it's too late, but how young are you suppose be? So don't wait around until it's too late! You are never too young or too old or too early to start a plan. By now, it should be sinking in, and that's GOOD! Now go back and do your "Napkin on the Fridge" and stick it right on the front of your fridge so you can start knowing your numbers by heart. Now is the time to write it up, review it, and know it... no matter how old you are.

The sooner you tackle your "Napkin on the Fridge" the better. You can begin saving now and cutting out the things that you really don't need. Start doing things that will add value to your I-Plan so you will be able to enjoy your glory years in the future.

When you decide to begin taking action and start setting aside money for your retirement, it is important that you have a plan on how you are going to build it, grow it and protect it. There are many tax incentives to saving, so work with an accountant and financial advisor to evaluate establishing a plan that will take advantage of all the tax savings incentives made available to you for establishing your retirement plan. Make sure you are always looking at the strategies and various vehicles that are designed to maximize your investments and money while minimizing as much tax as possible.

The three most popular tax-advantaged plans are IRAs, 401(k)s and retirement annuities.

Before we discuss these let's examine two important tax qualifications for your money. Keep in mind that I will not elaborate on them, we just need to know the basic difference, because most of us were never taught this. But, before we can understand retirement vehicles going forward we must understand the important difference between...

Non-qualified Money vs. Qualified Money

Non-qualified money: after-tax money that has already been taxed and then invested, and only the gain will be taxable as either ordinary income or capital gain depending on the type of investment vehicle you set up.

Qualified money: pre-taxed money that has never been taxed and invested into a retirement vehicle, and will be taxable as ordinary income when you begin taking withdrawals.
Now, let's look at the standard retirement vehicles.

Traditional IRAs (individual retirement accounts, qualified money) are for retirement purposes only. They allow individuals who are not otherwise covered by a pension plan or 401lk plan (aka a company or organization's retirement plan), and who make less than a certain amount of income, to set aside between $5,000 to $6,000 a year (depending that year's tax law and your age), tax-deferred annually, and allow to deduct your annual contribution from your annual income.

Each year, age, and income will vary the amounts allowable for you to set aside by law

That means that you don't pay taxes on the money you contribute towards your traditional IRA that year, because you can deduct that amount from your income instead.

You will be required to pay income tax on the money you withdraw as it will be included as part of your income that year you begin taking withdrawals. If you decide to withdraw money before 59 ½ you will also be subject to a 10% penalty on the amount you earned over the years.

Most traditional IRAs are tax deductible; meaning the money you pay into it each and every year is not counted towards your income.

The tax advantages normally disappear when your adjusted gross income exceeds certain amounts for individuals and couples. However, a traditional IRA is still an appealing way for you to set aside money as it compounds annually tax-deferred (meaning your interest grows without paying taxes until you begin taking withdrawals).

Roth IRAs are not tax deductible; the money grows tax-deferred and is NOT taxable when you begin taking withdrawals after the age of 59 ½.

Remember, it is important that you speak with your tax professional and financial advisor to determine your age/income and whether a Roth IRA or traditional IRA is suitable for your situation.

Roth IRAs & traditional IRAs can invest in a broad spectrum of investments and not limited to mutual funds, CDs, bank savings accounts, stocks, bonds, real estate, variable/fixed annuities, commodities, or a combination of these investment options.

While IRAs, and their cousins, the spousal IRA, SEP-IRA, and Keogh plan, are relatively simple, they are also just as strict. There is a 10% penalty on money withdrawn before you are age 59 $\frac{1}{2}$ from all IRAs and retirement vehicles alike, so make sure you are working with a tax professional and competent/qualified financial advisor before setting up such a plan for yourself and family.

RMD (Required Minimum Distribution) Once you reach the age of 70 $\frac{1}{2}$ you will be required by law to take a mandatory distribution from your traditional IRA that will be calculated for you based on your age (life expectancy) and marital status as well as the previous year's December 31st account value. You will be required each year after to take a distribution and as you get older the percentage will be higher, as our favorite Uncle Sam wants to make sure he gets his tax money back on the money you never paid over the years while investing in your traditional IRA.

The good news for those who have a Roth IRA, is that you will not be required to take an RMD, and any withdrawals you do decide to take or pass on, will always grow and allowed to be withdrawn TAX FREE after age 59 $\frac{1}{2}$ and upon your death allowed to be passed on to your heirs TAX FREE.

Please be careful of banks or those people trying to sell you the product of the month. THIS IS VERY IMPORTANT! I love and respect people working hard to make a living, but you're working just as hard and it's your money. All too often, I see young, old and wise going into a bank and walking out with a product or retirement vehicle that may not be suitable for their specific situation. This is very frustrating to see!

This is another good example you might have experienced yourself at sometime. I walk into the bank and they see my checking or my savings account and say "Hey Mr. Money, we see your savings account or checking account has now grown and you have not been using it. Would you like to sit down with a financial expert?" Now you tell me, what is a financial expert doing working for my local bank? I thought banks provide savings and checking accounts and offer CDs and loans, now they sell insurance and do investments too, really?

So I decide, hey why not? Let's entertain these people because I think they are going to give me a $50 gift certificate or a new coffee machine that I could really use. So I am going to listen to see what they have to say.

"So Mr. Money, do you have an IRA? Do you have an annuity? Do you have life insurance? How about if I told you if we set one up for you today because you are the PREMIER OF OUR MOST PREMIER CUSTOMERS, we are going to give you a SPECIAL interest rate or the lowest premium that no other bank today can provide, would you be interested?" Of course like most people I'd probably say, "Heck YEAH, I am the PREMIER OF PREMIEREST CUSTOMERS, my mom banked here, my dad banked here, my boss banks here, heck the government even tells me they even will guarantee my money if I bank here, so sign me up!"

Next thing you know I walk out, and now I have an IRA and a CD and/or a life insurance policy that I can't touch for who knows how long, but best of all I got a FREE DINNER and I got a free coffee machine, YEAH! Plus I am the PREMIER OF PREMIEREST CUSTOMERS THIS BANK HAS.

But one thing I forgot to ask, was what if I need that money tomorrow, what happens?

Okay, don't take me so seriously my lovers of banks, but the reality is the government does not GUARANTEE investments or insurance products at ANY bank, and more importantly does that banker even really know you and your situation? Do they know your goals or what is on your "Napkin on the Fridge?" Why do you think they always have a "Product of the Month" special? That's right, now you're thinking on the right track! A bank is a bank, your banker works for the bank, and not YOU!

So no matter who it is or how nice, cute or convincing they are, always ask "What if I need my money back tomorrow, what happens then?"

Ever wonder why it seems that there is a new financial expert or manager at your bank every few months? Why is that?

Now that I got that off my chest, let me take a breath, and tell you banks are there to make money while serving our everyday financial needs.

You're reading this book to learn how to make money for YOU, not the bank, not anyone else but YOU and YOUR family, so use the many green nuggets I have provided for you to think twice and do your homework before jumping into any financial transaction with a bank or anyone else for that matter.

Got it? Alright then, let's move on to 401(k) plans.

401(k) plan is a benefit many companies offer their employees, which allows you to participate in your own 401(k) (aka retirement account).

Green Nugget: If you don't work for a company and own your own business or are self-employed, you can establish your own 401(k) for yourself and or your employees. Keep in mind that there are many advantages and disadvantages in doing so for certain individuals and companies, so it would be best to seek professional financial and tax guidance before setting one up.

A 401(k) (qualified money) allows a worker to set aside a certain amount from their paycheck that will be able to grow tax-deferred. Many companies will even add or match that amount you contribute at NO COST to you, that's right! FREE MONEY! Some employers will match dollar for dollar up to a certain percentage of your income that you put aside.

The money can be invested in whatever investment vehicles the 401(k) plan provides, which are usually CDs, company stocks or bonds, mutual funds or annuities. Remember, each plan is different so review your 401(k) plan options to determine what is available to you. The nicest part about it is that you pay no tax until you withdraw it. Also, aside from the FREE MONEY MATCH, the other good news is that you get to deduct that amount from your income each year, reducing your tax liability to the government.

You can withdraw your 401(k) money without penalty when you retire or reach the age of $59\frac{1}{2}$, change jobs or become disabled. There is a 10% penalty however, for early withdrawals in most cases if made before age 59 $\frac{1}{2}$, unless you roll it over into your own IRA. Remember, you can deduct your contribution from your income each year, but when you do start taking a withdrawal, you will now have to add that withdrawal as part of your income that year, and will be required to pay taxes on that withdrawal.

That free money match mentioned earlier, grows tax-deferred, meaning you don't pay any taxes on the earnings each year until you begin withdrawals. It's a NO BRAINER RIGHT?

So there is no reason not to at least contribute the free money match percentage the company is offering you.

I am pretty sure the Frumpys have an example of this that we can learn from, let's check in.

Auntie Frida has been working at the Green Parrot Resort in Costa Rica for a long time.

She went through many financial problems while she was going through her divorce and even had to borrow money from her brother Fred for a while. After she paid him back, she started to concentrate on her "Napkin on the Fridge" and quickly began to wonder if she will ever be able to retire.

Fortunately for Frida, Green Parrot Resort has a 401(k) plan available to its employees and even matches dollar for dollar up to 4% of her annual pay if she contributes to the plan.

Let's break it down so it's easier to see.

Frida's Income: $50,000 per year

Multiply her income of $50,000 x 4% = $2,000

Her Contribution: $2,000

Her FREE money MATCH from the Resort: $2,000

That means the total contribution to be deducted from her taxes that year and be put aside towards her retirement: $2000 her contribution +$2000 Green Parrot Resort free money match (which she cannot deduct from her taxes that year) = $4000 (which she can set aside towards her retirement 401(k)).

Auntie Frida elected to participate in her plan at the least amount of percentage her employer will match dollar for dollar. Her financial advisor and tax professional told Auntie Frida that tax regulations cap how much she can contribute to her 401(k) plan in order to be able to write it off from her yearly income.

Auntie Frida also asked her financial advisor and tax professional if she could contribute more than

4% a year. She thinks she can save more now that she has her "Napkin on the Fridge" and let's not forget that she broke up with all her surfer boyfriends!

Her financial advisor said she may want to contribute 10% of her pay to her 401(k) plan, but in this scenario, her employer will still only match her contribution dollar for dollar up to 4%. Remember, each plan will differ and the best way to find out about your company's plan is to ask your benefits manager at the company you work for.

In Auntie Frida's situation, let's say she will be contributing 10% towards her 401(k) and her income is $50,000 per year (.10 x $50,000) = $5,000.

The FREE money match from Auntie Frida's employer, The Green Parrot Resort, is still only 4% of $50,000, which is $2,000.

So the total contribution to her 401(k) would be $7,000 ($5000 her contribution + $2000 free money match). Keep in mind, her $5,000 contribution would be deducted from her taxes that year, but the $2,000 money match would not).

However if you are planning to save more in your 401(k) like Auntie Frida is considering, then check with your tax professional and financial advisor to analyze your situation enough to know how much you should be contributing, if you qualify or if it's advantageous based on your income to participate.

Again, I want to stress that you need to work with your professional financial and tax advisors to analyze where you are in life, your "Napkin on the Fridge," your family's needs, your savings, your goals and all of your concerns, before setting up your 401(k). However, no matter what, if it's a FREE money match, DO IT! Whatever the percentage is that your company plan will provide you, allocate at least that percentage from your paycheck. You can worry about the consequences later, if there are any, but for now FREE MONEY is FREE MONEY and if you don't take advantage of this benefit, you lose it. Got it?

Annuities: can be used for many purposes and can be within a qualified retirement vehicle or set up as a non-qualified retirement vehicle, but because of their tax advantages they are popular supplements to retirement plans. The tax advantages of annuities are that you pay no tax on interest or capital gains earned until you begin to receive payouts. To keep it simple, just understand that annuities are backed by an insurance carrier and provide guarantees, but they also allow for someone to set up their own (for example a pension) and contribute as much as you'd like with no limits depending on the plan and insurance company's requirements. Remember, they can be within a qualified plan IRA, 401(k), pension plan or as your own stand-alone non-qualified plan after tax set up.

Annuities are probably the most misunderstood vehicles among advisors, professionals, the media, agents, analysts and others.

One annuity tactic that I dislike the most is the "Bait & Switch" annuity tactic. You hear a radio ad or see a newspaper advertisement telling you how bad annuities are, "don't ever do an annuity the sky will start falling if you set up one up."

So you call to find out more or meet with that person who advertised how bad annuities were, and what do you know, you end up walking out with an annuity. Funny, isn't it? But it's true.They had to get you in the door somehow, and because they know a competent advisor will help you evaluate whether an annuity should be part of your plan or not. So as soon as you hear how bad they are, of course they know you will you want to know why.

I am not sure why annuities are so misunderstood, they are pretty straight forward. The definition, however, isn't so straight forward.

Annuity - income from capital investment paid in a series of regular payments. So what are they exactly? They are basically a pension backed by an insurance carrier, guaranteeing you a lifetime income stream based on a variety of factors including the type of annuity product, your age, the option you choose and the interest rate at the time of election.

The nicest thing about an annuity, is that it provides guarantees, and we love guarantees, but don't forget if it sounds too good to be true it normally is. That is why it's important to understand the various annuity vehicles you can elect from and the purpose and differences between them. Never forget that each of our situations are different, so maybe an annuity is good for one but is not suitable for another. So when you hear someone making a blanket statement like "Oh, annuities are terrible, you should never get an annuity," I can assure you they are most likely saying this because they don't understand annuities or they won't make any money from it or it's just not in THEIR best interest if you set one up. I love how those that bash annuities, usually always say "the FEES are HIGH" or "you are going to pay big commissions to the broker." The reality is, people need to get paid, what does that have to do with you? Do you really think if you put that money into a vehicle that is NOT an annuity with that advisor/banker/planner or whomever, is not going to get paid well?

Ask anyone who had a pension when they retired from their job, a teacher, a professor, a union worker, government official, or anyone you know that has a pension. Ask them if they do or don't like their pension? Are they paying way to high fees and the broker made tons of commissions? I mean really ask them. Get the answer for yourself, don't let this book or any other book or professional tell you what's right for you, find out for yourself. In reality, an annuity is a pension that has guarantees, so ask your advisor or financial planner or whoever you are working with, does their plan provide guarantees backed by an insurance company? Would you rather pay fees for guarantees or no fees for no guarantees?

Now, it's time to take a look at the different annuity vehicles that are out there. This will help you understand there are differences, and better yet after you understand, maybe you can even educate those experts on why annuities can be so good. I can't tell you from experience how many times I have met with an accountant, attorney, planner, famous TV personalities or a professional that said, "Oh annuities are bad...bad...bad." As I said before, talk to those who do have a pension, and see how they felt when the markets tanked. I can assure you those with an annuity didn't lose any sleep. Why? Because they paid those so-called high fees and commissions, but guess what? Their annuity came with guarantees; ah we do love those guarantees. So maybe paying for fees with guarantees really does make sense. Who knows? Only you know your situation enough to properly determine whether they make sense for you or not, just don't be scared into or out of any retirement, investment, or insurance vehicle. Instead do your homework and ask questions, and yes even though it sounds boring you must read the fine print.

Think of it this way. Have you ever put together something you bought using instructions? Or should I say bought something that had instructions, but you decided you didn't need them, and just needed the pictures to be able to put it together? We have all done it. By nature, we like things easy and simple. Now ask yourself, how long it took you to put that product together? How many times did you put one leg upside down or backwards or forward, left or right, and next thing you knew you wanted to send it back to the store because it didn't come with all the parts. I know you've been there.

However, in the end you were smart enough to take the product apart and start over because you were too lazy to bring it back to the store or send it back. This time you instead decided, well I will just read and follow along with the instructions and see what happens.

The majority of times like this, the product came together with no problems and turned out exactly how it looked in the picture, right? Okay there ARE those times, especially when the product was made in China, they forgot a screw or something. At least you didn't need to send it back or bring back that monster package, you just needed that one piece that was left out by the careless worker who boxed your item and didn't do a thorough check before shipping it out.

Are you following me? The point is, when you read the fine print and you take a few extra minutes out of your day to follow along, what do you know, good things usually happen. So think of your retirement annuity, investments, insurances, and other financial matters as products, follow the instructions and read the fine print. This will give you the answers and questions necessary for you and your advisors and give you the peace of mind knowing that your neighbor, family member, friend, or advisor are only telling you otherwise because they didn't read the instructions like you did.

There are two different types of annuities:

Immediate annuity and Deferred annuity

Immediate annuities begin providing income as soon as the contract is set up. You use an annuity when you want to provide a guaranteed income stream for life.

Deferred annuities do not begin making payments until a later date. You contribute to this type of annuity expecting, and allowing, the cash to grow over time. This gives you the opportunity to have a higher income payout when you decide to turn it on and begin receiving income.

For example, the years you are working and contributing to your annuity/pension, the longer you work and contribute the more cash that builds and the more income you will have available when you retire.

Is an annuity a pension?

An annuity is another term for pension, which is a retirement vehicle contributed to over a period of time accumulating to provide a specific income stream for the remainder of one's life. The person who contributes to a pension will have various options to choose from when the time comes when they are able or want to turn it on as a lifetime income stream.

Pensions have become a thing of the past, and over the years have been replaced by 401(k) plans. This is now putting more pressure on YOU to make sure you are contributing to your own retirement account, whereas in years past the company was putting the money away for you.

Here's another Green Nugget: That is very important for your glory years. Analysts and economists suggest that you make sure you are contributing a minimum of 15-18%

of your annual salary towards a retirement vehicle such as an IRA, 401(k), pension or annuity, in order to be able to enjoy the same levels of income you are receiving now, when you finally decide to hang it up and enjoy your glory years, meaning retire. Do I agree with this? Can we argue this, of course we can, but it is a good benchmark to consider and work with when evaluating your retirement plan.

I want to stress once more that we are all in different situations, so just like your I-Plan, remember what the "I" stands for, "YOU!" Your plan is not anyone else's but yours, so take control and use this information as a foundation to help you achieve success. You must always be willing to be flexible in order to learn and make the necessary adjustments as your situation will continue to change as you move on along your life's journey.

Now that we understand immediate vs. deferred, let's examine the different annuity products or options we can choose from within an annuity.

Fixed Annuity, Variable Annuity and Equity Indexes Annuity

Fixed annuities: are very simple and straight forward. The insurance company you establish the contract with provides a guaranteed interest rate on the money you put in at the time you set up the contract. This will establish a guarantee on the earnings and the principal for a period of time stipulated by the contract terms. You can turn it into an immediate annuity at some point whenever you decide or continue to defer it and allow your money to grow tax-deferred at a fixed interest rate.

The definition of fixed annuity is in fact, an annuity in which payments to the annuitant are unchanging over a specified period or over the annuitant's lifetime.

133

Variable annuities: the rate of return is not stable in variable annuities, and will vary with the performance of the stock, bond and money market investment options you choose within. There are no guarantees on the return on your investments within and there is the risk that you might lose money. Unlike fixed annuity contracts, variable annuities are securities that are registered with the Securities and Exchange Commission due to the fact there are investments inside the contract that determine your rate of return.

The biggest difference between a fixed and a variable annuity is the possibility of "extra" income from stock, bond, or mutual fund price increases inside the variable annuity verses a fixed interest rate guaranteed and back by the insurance carrier in a fixed annuity. Just like a fixed annuity, variable annuities can offer you a guaranteed income for life, pending your contract options.

The definition of a variable annuity is an annuity in which payments to the annuitant can vary according to the changing market value of the underlying investment.

Equity-Indexed Annuities: are more complex financial instruments that have characteristics of both fixed and variable annuities.

The definition of an Equity-Indexed annuity is an annuity with an interest rate linked to the performance of some index (i.e. S&P 500).

Again, I continue to stress to you, see a professional who understands all annuity products and their options and can further explain the details of all three, and which one might best suit your situation and goals.

Annuities can be more flexible if they are set up outside of your IRA/401(k) (qualified money). You can invest all your money at once (single premium annuity), or at regular intervals, as long as it is set up outside of your Qualified Plan (IRA/401(k) plan), as mentioned, classified as after-tax money (non-qualified).

On the plus side, there are many types of annuities that are offered by insurance carriers, so you will have many options to choose from. Remember, when evaluating its most important to work with someone that not only can educate you on the different types available, but can also provide you analysis from all the carriers offering them, not just a select few.

Real Estate: can also be considered another vehicle for retirement. Although many people saw the real estate bubble burst, real estate can be another investment vehicle to prepare for retirement.

This can be true for both residential and commercial real estate.

Real estate can appreciate in value, and provide income if you rent it out. The tenant(s), over time, can help you pay off the mortgage before you retire. This would allow the real estate to provide an additional income stream in retirement if it continues to be rented during retirement.

It is important to consider your experience in buying real estate as well as the decision about being a landlord should you choose to use this vehicle for retirement savings.

Which one should you choose? I have two valuable tips to help you decide:

There is no one size fits all.

Diversify, diversify, diversify!

Disclosure: Diversification does not protect against a loss in a declining market.

Chapter XXII

Diversification

The best way to invest is invest a little bit in various investments or insurance backed vehicles. Like the good old saying goes "never have all of your eggs in one basket." Always look to take advantage of the tax strategies and incentives available with each plan or investment.

Speaking to an independent financial advisor or planner would be a good idea, as always, and make sure to interview a few different accountants or CPAs. They can help point you in the right direction according to your needs, goals and concerns.

I think it's time we check in with the Frumpys. Granny Frumpy, as you learned earlier, is a savvy business woman. She is the real estate icon of the Frumpy Family.

She started buying real estate at very young age and she knows money does not grow on trees. She has been trying to teach this to Frank for quite a while. It took Granny Frumpy many persistent years of hard work and learning from mistakes to get to where she is now.

Granny Frumpy has many assets and great cash flow (income). But she knows diversification is the best way to protect her and her money in case something happens to one of her investments.

At first, Granny Frumpy did not understand annuities, but after speaking with her financial advisor he encouraged that she consider this option.
So Granny Frumpy decided to add one as part of her I-Plan. She knows annuities in her state of Florida, as well as in many other states, are protected against creditors or those "haters" that are always trying to sue her.

She met with her financial advisor to put an estate plan together. She wanted to make sure her assets are fully protected. Also, she wants to make sure her legacy will last for generations to come.

After meeting with her advisor, her tax professional and her attorney, Granny Frumpy asked if they could meet with Uncle Floyd as well.

She is always worried about the way Uncle Floyd treats his money, but even more worried about the people he associates with, especially all those different Honeys he has that change from week to week.

She thinks Uncle Floyd needs to consider establishing some annuities to help secure and protect a pension for his future before he blows all his money like many of his celebrity friends or before some "want-to-be baby momma" finds some money hungry attorney to sue him for his money.

Annuities may provide Uncle Floyd some guaranteed income for his life and protect him against lawsuits, creditors and baby mommas, as well as the ups and downs of the market.

Granny Frumpy is going to insist Uncle Floyd learn more about annuities. She wants to have the peace of mind knowing she helped him secure his future income when he is no longer able to fight.

After doing her homework, Granny Frumpy can now explain annuities easily to Uncle Floyd:

Annuities = Income for life, also guaranteed and protected against creditors (in many states).

If Uncle Floyd needs more explanation she will make sure he at least gets a second opinion from her "star team" of experts.

Take advantage of Free Money

Free Money? NO there is NO truly free money in life. However, there are tax advantages available to you for your retirement plan where you pay little or no tax on your money while it is grows.

Of course, all of us have to pay taxes when we make money. I don't like it, and you won't like it, no one likes it, but it's just a part of life. The more money you make the more taxes you pay. However, there are many strategies and incentives made available to all of us to help lessen those taxes or defer them to be paid at a later date. Let's take a look.

Tax advantages and incentives:

This is when taxes are not paid on your money or earnings today but are invested and deferred until you decide to withdraw the money or earnings from that particular account. Withdrawals may consist of contributions and accumulated earnings that will be taxable.

If you were to invest in certain types of accounts, these vehicles would allow your money to grow and can be withdrawn tax free provided certain requirements are met.

There are various types of tax-advantage accounts.

We previously discussed the differences between retirement vehicles, such as Roth IRAs vs traditional IRAs. There are many different tax-advantaged accounts including individual retirement accounts, Traditional IRAs, Roth IRAs, retirement annuities and employer-sponsored retirement plans (401(k) plan & pension plan) just to name some of the more standard and basic ones most of us have available.

Each account type has its own rules that govern contribution limits and eligibility requirements. Also, keep in mind that tax penalties may apply for withdrawals made prior to reaching age $59\frac{1}{2}$.

The more money you make, the more taxes you will pay. This is where working with expert advisors that specialize in tax planning will be beneficial in making your decision. You will be amazed at what billionaires will do when it comes to tax planning, there are many tools in the toolbox designed to lessen the tax burdens placed on us as well as the super-rich, so if you are interested in learning about these types of strategies, no book is going to do it for you, you'll need to work with experts in this field.

How about other tax incentives/advantages available to all of us?

There are plenty of tax deductions out there just waiting to be found.

Most tax deductions center around those areas that are part of life, such as medical costs, buying a home, having children, earning a living, getting an education and helping people who are less fortunate.

Below are some areas for you to consider when looking for deductions. It is worthwhile to review these carefully and make sure you are within the IRS guidelines. Then, you should review them with your tax professional.

Medical expenses: Need to total at least 7.5 percent of your adjusted gross income (AGI) in order for you to take the medical expense deduction on your early income. You can deduct medical-related expenses that exceed those covered by your insurance plan or are not accepted by your insurance plan. For example, glasses, contact lenses, braces, false teeth, lab fees, emergency room visits, travel to and from medical treatments, medical supplies and laser surgery are all potential medical deductions.

How are those Frumpys doing? Flea is doing much better. He survived all his medical issues and his cancer has gone into remission. It has been very stressful mentally and financially dealing with all the doctors, hospitals and bills.

Flea sees life in a different way now. He feels like he has been born again.

The bad part of the story is that he racked up a very large medical bill; while part of it was covered by his insurance, a large part had to come out of his own pocket.

These days the health care costs are unbelievably high. They can break your piggy bank. Fortunately, Flea was always smart enough to have an emergency fund set up. He is also hopeful that a large portion of his medical expenses will be deductible against his taxes; but this is something he has yet to discuss with his tax professional.

Work-related expenses: May include uniforms or specific clothing necessary for your job, business travel expenses and the many costs associated with a work-related relocation. Be careful and make sure to follow the IRS guidelines that define what is used for business purposes.

The Frumpys can show us an example of this too.

Fran has become a workaholic since her dad passed away. She was promoted at FrumpySoft and hopes to someday run the company. Fran feels it's her calling to carry on her dad's legacy.

She barely even has time to shop these days.

Poor Fonzie, every day when Fran gets home, she is so tired that she doesn't have the energy to play with him. Fonzie is alone all day, but Fran makes sure to spend as much time as she can during the weekends to keep Fonzie active.

For the first time, Fran asked her mom, Flo, to buy some dresses for her because she doesn't have the time to shop anymore. Her new position requires her to be well dressed, and hopes she can write off some of the clothing she purchases since they are required for her new position at work.

Homeowners: Mortgage interest payments are deductible. Therefore, if your mortgage interest is higher than your standard deduction, speak with your tax advisor to itemize and take advantage of the greater deduction.

Fran is also able to write off the interest on her mortgage that she has been paying on her new house. Fonzie is so happy in his new place! He is the king of the castle! He sleeps all day long, eats, plays with his bones and sleeps some more until his momma comes home and he is always excited for the weekends, what a life!

Child Tax Credit: As of 2011, if your income is below $110,000 per year, you will receive $1,000 per child as a tax credit. If you are adopting, you will receive up to $13,700 tax credit per child, but there are income limitations as well up to $187,520-$222,520 (discuss the up to date laws with a tax professional).

Looks like there is more drama going on with the Frumpys. Uncle Floyd just found out he is having a baby! Oh know who's the Baby Mama? Everybody knew this was going to happen.

Fortunately for Floyd, it's with his long time girlfriend, the beautiful actress Fofina, and she is due next week!

However, Uncle Floyd will NOT receive the $2,000 tax credit. Why $2000? The couple is having twins, but since Floyd makes over $110,000 a year, he does not qualify. Floyd may not worry about $2000 now, but as time goes on Granny Frumpy continues to teach him that every penny counts.

Charitable deductions: Make sure you have a receipt or statement of the value of goods donated if your donation is in the form of goods or services rather than cash.

Flo donated all of Fred's clothing to the Salvation Army. This was a very nice gesture and she may be able to get a charitable tax deduction from our favorite uncle, Uncle Sam.

Good for her!

Education deductions: Include tuition and enrollment fees to accredited public or private institutions above the high school level. They can be deducted on your behalf or on the behalf of your spouse or your dependents, after deducting the portion paid by college financial assistance or scholarships. There also financial instruments that will assist in various tax-deductions depending the state you live in.

Is Frank going to college?

He has not decided yet. But Flo knows that she may be able to receive some tax deductions or credits for some of the tuition fees if Frank decides to pursue higher education.

There are many other tax advantages and incentives out there, too many in fact to discuss in just one chapter, but what is most important to take away from all this is to make sure you keep all your receipts and discuss your situation and concerns with a qualified tax professional.

In today's high tech, fast paced society, there are many online sources, apps and highly popular tax software programs that allow you to do your taxes on your own. From experience, working with someone whose sole focus is taxes and stays current with the many changes to the tax system, will be very beneficial to you. When working with a professional you might find that the more complex your job, financial structure, family structure, or income is the more beneficial it is to work with them. These professionals can help you take advantage of all the tax incentives and strategies that are available to you.

Green Nugget: Never ASSUME!!!

I know you know what they say when you ASSUME something...

Why do I say this? Just because a person is a CPA, tax accountant, tax planner or tax attorney, does not mean they are current with the changes that have been made to the tax code in that particular year. So as you should have learned by now, do your own homework, do your own research. The internet has become a powerful educational tool, so use it to your advantage. You will be surprised when you actually question these professionals, just how often they make mistakes, so don't just trust they are qualified and precise, ask questions and NEVER ASSUME they know everything.

Chapter XXIII
Importance of your STAR TEAM

You might be thinking, "WOW...this is all too overwhelming, way too many things to know and learn, I don't have time, I don't really care, I have to work, I have a business to run, I have to run my practice, I have to pass these exams, I have to take care of my family, I have my own things to do, come on now!"

Whatever your reason is, it is why I always advise people to build a strong team. If you have a good team of qualified dedicated professionals, they will help you avoid paying for mistakes.

To have a team of professionals means you can focus on what's important to you and be able to work with peace of mind. You do not have to worry about things that are not in your field of expertise, such as new tax laws or incentives that the government just passed, or how to structure your Estate (all assets owned by you) in order to protect it against law suits or Uncle Sam. As a result you can perform better at what you do best and concentrate on how you can make more money, take care of your health and your family.

Example: Let's say you are a physician. Realistically, you would not have time to think about how the market is doing, let alone analyze it and manage your own portfolio by yourself. On top of that you just might not have the skills for it!

I am not a handyman myself. I would rather hire a professional to perform some work I need instead of doing it myself. I know the professional will perform the job well because he has the skills for it. Spend money wisely.

Green Nugget: Time is Money

This means if you can spend your time wisely on things that can bring you money or happiness, then you are saving the time, which also equals money. Trying to figure it out yourself can waste time and money. Spend your time only to research the basics in order to make sure the professionals you are working with have your best interest at heart and are not costing you money for their incompetence or dishonesty.

Your Star Team

For your financial success you should interview three professionals to be part of your "Star Team."

It may take some time before you find the right professionals to be part of your "Star Team," because like in any business finding good people you can trust is very difficult. Do not give up! At some point, after hiring and firing many different team members, you will see you finally put together the best "Star Team!" And they will make things much easier for you, saving you time equaling more...money? Time to spend with family? Time enjoying your hobby? Now you're getting it!

Your team should consist of an independent financial advisor or planner, a certified public accountant (CPA) or tax accountant and an attorney that has the resources that are needed to refer you to more specialized attorneys if needed.

Independent Financial Advisor or Planner

An independent financial advisor or planner that also has

access to an insurance professional, can work with you to establish a game plan for the future so that you can manage your debt in a better way, optimize your tax structure, have a solid asset protection plan in place, make best use of retirement investment vehicles and opportunities, maintain adequate liquidity and having adequate protections in place to prevent any adverse financial circumstances.

Also, make sure your advisor is independent, meaning he or she is not working for a bank and they are able to provide you as many options available in the market according to your needs and goals.

Consider working with an advisor that is a fiduciary advisor, which means an independent financial advisor, or someone held to a "Fiduciary Standard" special trust and confidence when working for a client. As a fiduciary, the financial advisor is required to act with undivided loyalty to the client. This includes disclosure of how the financial advisor is to be compensated and any corresponding conflicts of interest.

A CPA or Tax Accountant: Your "tax guy"

Many people think they do not need a CPA or a tax accountant. Like the majority of Americans, you might think you have a good handle on completing your taxes on your own, thanks to software systems and services available both on and offline.

But do you really have enough knowledge to take complete advantage of the complex tax code, which changes every year? What if your financial situation is more complex than you think? Maybe you really are that smart and have the time, but why not confirm you are, especially if it will help put more money on your napkin at the end of the year.

Sometimes when you think you are saving, you may not know you are missing many other incentives or changes made to the tax code that year. All because you might not have the knowledge you thought you did or taxes are not your specialty. Remember those Green Nuggets...

"Spend money to make money."

"Spend pennies to protect dollars."

If you have specialized or complicated tax returns, it will probably be worth it to pay a professional. Even if you believe you don't, take the time to find out if it is true.

Attorney/Lawyer

I don't know where to start when it comes to making sure you have an attorney or a lawyer on your team. I just know at some point in your life, you need a will or an estate plan, so you may need to have an attorney or lawyer, and ready to pay!! The good news, there are unique ways now to draw up your own will, that is much less costly. I have even seen cases in which people have made their own wills with the information and programs that are available online, and established a video that described their final wishes. Now that's a green nugget!

Will: A will is a document that you draw up to determine what your final wishes are on how you would like to distribute your assets at the time of your death.

There are many different types of attorneys, and some can charge LOTS of money. So this is where you really need to do your homework before determining if you really need one. They say 50% of the people who get married will end up getting divorced, so divorce attorneys must be making a killing right? Well, maybe then it's wise that you consider mitigation before going to the courts or an attorney. So think wisely before hiring legal counsel and be very careful in making sure you find out their fees ahead of time. NO MATTER HOW ANGRY YOU ARE!

Some attorneys work by the hour or charge a flat fee, or a fee based on a percentage of your case.

The most important thing you must realize is that an attorney does not know it all, sometimes they may act like they do, but those are the ones you need to be careful of. Instead, they all have their own specialties, so first evaluate your needs and make sure the attorney or lawyer you work with is specialized to handle your situation.

Green Nugget: If your attorney doesn't call you back or is constantly charging you unnecessary fees, you have the right to fire him or her and have them provide a detailed explanation of those fees/charges in writing.

You will often times find that attorneys and lawyers are held to a higher standard from their BAR Association in their particular state, so never hesitate to hold them accountable to your situation. Just because your estate is worth 1 million dollars does not mean it takes any more time for them to draw up a basic document than the guy or gal whose estate is worth $100,000 or $10,000. Ask questions and do your own research, and that goes for any professional you are working with, your financial advisor or planner, insurance professional, CPA/accountant, attorney, contractor, plumber, electrician, professor, teacher, coach, mentor...whoever it may be.

Make sure you choose your "Star Team" wisely. Choose each member of your team based on their qualifications, their knowledge, experience, and the way you feel about them (trust and feel comfortable and confident when working with them, test them to make sure they have your best interests at heart and NOT your "healthy pockets'").

The Frumpy Family now has their own "Star Team"

in place. This team took Fred many years to build. Fortunately, with the encouragement from Fred's financial advisor, Fred Frumpy and his "Star Team" decided to build a family trust a year before he passed away. It was not easy and it took some time for him to find qualified people he could trust. He knew that this team would take care of his assets and, most importantly his family when he would not be able to do it himself anymore.

Fred always worked with his independent financial advisor, CPA and business/estate planning attorney to make sure all his goals and wishes would be coordinated and protected.

When Fred passed away, Flo was surrounded by Fred's qualified and well-trusted team. The team continues to advise her and make sure that the family is well protected.

Even Uncle Floyd decided to interview the "Star Team" and agreed to work with them for his asset protection and investment management. Now that he has two kids, Floyd has more responsibilities than he ever had before in regard to his family's future. He never knows when the day will come that he will no longer be able to fight, time is not on his side.

Chapter XXIV

Retirement Number

I must confess, that even though you are now on track with your I-Plan and have your "Napkin on the Fridge" in place, there is something that I must tell you. Not everything will go as planned for everybody. So please, do not get discouraged or quit...ever. Quitting is not an option, even if your plan does not work out the way you envisioned. You must always remember there will be bumps in the road on your journey, but you will always be able to get back on track if you believe and put your mind and soul behind it. Most importantly put your plan and your goals on paper and put your plan into every day practice.

You have to see "it" and believe "it" every day, for "it" to become your reality.

Now let's talk about your retirement number, but only if you want to retire. Do you want to hit 60 years old and still be working an 8 to 5 or whatever your standard hours are? Maybe you do. Maybe you own a business and never want to retire, because you love it too much. I am a big believer that if you love what you do and you are making money at it, it's really not a J O B, its L I V I N G.

Though many of us would like to be at least semi-retired, others of us would like to be 100% RETIRED.

So tell me, at what age do you want to be relaxing on the beach with your wifey or hubby? Traveling with your BFF, playing golf, or fishing, or dancing or living every day as like it is a party, doing whatever it is you enjoy? Think of all the dreams you can see yourself enjoying without work right now. If you could pick a realistic age at which to retire, what would it be? At what age can you see yourself putting on the brakes in life to finally have the chance to enjoy the reward of all your hard working years? Imagine you can now enjoy things you always wanted to do, day in and day out, WITHOUT WORKING.

Good news, you can get there someday or you might be there now, but to be there, and really enjoy it, you need a plan and using your I-Plan is a great way to reach your goals.

Without a plan, forget it! You will be the one relying on the government in hopes that Social Security will still be around, but be honest with yourself, is this really the route you want to take?

Like many, you might think you have no choice, but I am here to tell you, YOU DO HAVE CHOICES! Make today a day of action and do NOT GIVE UP, NEVER GIVE UP, dig deep and find the WILL to WIN no matter what odds your mind tells you, you are up against.

It's not the chances we take, but the choices we make in life that determine our destiny.

How to know your retirement number?

The way I am going to explain it may sound very simple, but in reality it really is that simple. All you need to do is figure out how much you will need to live on in any given year. If you have done your "Napkin on The Fridge," then you should already have a very good idea as to how much you need during an average year.

You can add some expenses for trips and other stuff so you can make your retirement more enjoyable and comfortable.

Let's say your number is $70,000 per year.

$70,000 is what you need in a year to cover all your expenses with a little cushion just to be safe against the unexpected. Make sure you cushion your number enough so you can live the way you want when you reach your retirement and your glory years.

So, if you need $70,000, take that number and divide it by .03, which is a very safe rate of return for your number. If you needed $70,000 a year in retirement that would mean:

70,000 / .03 = 2.333 million dollars is your number.

Say what? That's right! You will need 2.333 million dollars in order to be able to enjoy $70,000 a year for the rest of your life. Meaning you will have to accumulate 2.333 million dollars in retirement and savings to be able to enjoy $70,000 a year for the rest of your life.

Now you have to plan accordingly based your age at present and the age you want to retire to reach that number ($2,333,000).

Basically this will give a conservative number to be able live off the return of your investments for the remainder of your lifetime.

I am sure the Frumpys want to retire comfortably. What is Auntie Frida's number?

Her expenses per year give or take are $60,000 (she had to cut some shopping, some nights at the local bar, some beauty supplies at her favorite department store). But, she still wants to go for a cruise.

$60,000 / .03 = 1.8 million dollars

1.8 million dollars is her number.

4% Rule

There is a basic rule of thumb used by many financial advisers, called the 4% rule.

In retirement, you can withdraw 4% of your assets every year. This assumes your investments are returning an average of around 7 percent a year with a mixture of stocks and/or bonds and other investment options. A portion of each year's gains must remain invested to offset inflation, which hovers around 3% over the long term.

There are many retirement calculators online and now even apps like the "I-PLAN APP" for your SmartPhone that allows you to play with the numbers that fit your situation, so it doesn't have to physically be on the fridge. This way you can figure out how much you need to save to reach your number according to your age and your expenses.

Keep in mind, that when you retire, they normally say your expenses will go down, because your house is paid off, you have no kids to worry about and Social Security might kick in, but that doesn't necessarily mean your expenses won't go up either, right?

Living la vida loca, Five Star restaurants and hotels, first class travel, fine wine, luxury cars…whatever your heart and soul desires, just make sure you calculate it in your number. Who's to say you CAN'T or WON'T spend more money when you retire? I mean, now you have the time to really enjoy all those things money can buy, right?

I am not one who tells people what to do, my philosophy is "ENJOY LIFE TO THE FULLEST if it makes YOU HAPPY and YOU can AFFORD IT when you are RETIRED, WHY NOT?" Is your coffin going to have drawers? You can't take it with you!

There are many good retirement calculators that you can find online to help you with your number, so be sure to evaluate a few and search the term "retirement calculator."

If you are overwhelmed by all of this and all these numbers, you can talk with your financial advisor and the rest of your "Star Team" to help you to figure out your numbers with you. That's what they are there for, but at least you can now keep them in check with your knowledge and your realistic expectations.

Keep in mind:

It's never too early to start saving for retirement -- and never too late.

Always concentrate on things you can control.

Green Nugget: Rule of 72, is a very easy way to calculate in your head how long it will take to double your money based on a given fixed interest rate, assuming the interest is annually compounded.

All you have to do is divide 72 by the interest rate. The resulting number is the number of years it will take for the amount to double, given that fixed interest rate. For example: if you invest $10,000 in a CD paying 3% compounded annually, it would take about 72/3 = 24 years to turn that into $20,000. On the flip side, if you have same amount of debt, say $50,000 in student loans, at a 5% interest rate which you don't make payments on, it will take 72/5 = 14.4 years for the amount owed to double to $100,000.

You can also run the calculation the other way, if you want to determine what interest rate you'd need to double your money in a given amount of time. For instance: if you have $10,000 in savings and would like to double it in the next 10 years without adding anything to it, you'd need an interest rate of around 72/10 = 7.2%.

Chapter XXV

Protecting Assets for Your Family

Now that you've worked harder and smarter, you've built your empire. You may have a house or maybe even a couple of houses. You may have a successful business. You may have a good retirement plan. You may have a fat pink pig hidden in your basement (the kind filled with money, of course!).

Now it is time to protect it, for you, for your family and for the many generations to come. It is now your legacy of hard work and success to leave behind.

Do not let Uncle Sam take it from you. Do not let anybody take it from you.

Why would you?

There are many strategies to protect your assets, and the best way to do it is work with professionals that are skilled for it, aka your "Star Team."

Everybody has different goals, concerns, dreams and needs.

Prepare and structure your Estate Plan or business plan in the most efficient manner possible where your assets are protected from Uncle Sam and those that may have ill will towards you, so you can be proud to know you left a legacy that will live on for generations to come.

You do not want your assets unprotected in a way that

allows them to be cut in half by the government due to inheritance taxes when you die or see an ill-willed person or family member file a frivolous lawsuit to go after everything you've worked hard for.

Make sure that you have a will or trusts or other financial instruments or your company incorporated, so that all of the necessary documents are put in place while you are healthy and have your wits intact. These days, there are many free websites you can go to and do it yourself if you feel you do not need a lawyer to do it for you, but as your estate or business becomes more complex it is wise to hire specialized legal, financial and tax professionals to work with you and your family to protect your lifelong years of success.

Will: There is not a specific or required form. A legal will can simply be a statement; it can be like a letter or in the form of a legal document. The form or format used doesn't matter. There are not any specific words that must be used, but it must be clear to the person or persons making the "last will and testament," which means it will be effective upon his or her death.

You can say "upon my death," "when I die," or any similar wording. Simply saying "I give ___ to ___" will not work, nor will it be legally binding, because it sounds like any present or gift to be given at anytime, not a gift that is to be effective upon death. There is no requirement that an attorney must draft a last will and testament for you. A legal will must be signed by the person making the last will and it must also be signed by two or three competent adults who were present and witnessed the maker sign the last will. Most states require two witnesses, but some states require three witnesses. The witnesses must not be named in the last will. To be a fully legal will, the person making the last will and testament must be eighteen (18) years old or older, he or she must be making his or her last will voluntary, and he or she must be competent.

You may have heard of a trust being a form of asset protection, but if you haven't I will give you an idea of what it does and when it should be looked at.

Trust: A trust is a contract. It's as simple as that. You can't see it or touch it, but it becomes a separate legal entity. It is represented by a written trust agreement.

There are different types of trusts, but the main benefit of all trusts is that they will keep your estate out of probate courts after your death.

Probate courts are courts that have the jurisdiction to administer and validate the genuineness of a will and last testament or a trust.

When you create a trust you can transfer all of your property, assets, bank accounts, securities and real estate to a person or persons you "trust."

When a trust is done right, it will protect your assets in many ways. It can protect your assets from probate (attorneys and court fees) after your death. Trusts can also help save on estate taxes and keep all assets out of creditor's clutches. They can also keep your property away from a divorcee.

Your "Star Team" can give you many options on how to protect and save your money while protecting your family assets.

Complicated? Boring? Interesting?

It is part of your financial plan. Your dreams that you worked or working hard to come true must be protected for those you love.

Let's check in with the Frumpys. The other day, Frank asked Grandpa and Granny Frumpy if they had their wills set up yet. Frank has a lot of friends, and has seen some of his best ones fight with their families over money and inheritance.

Fred always said that when families fight, the people who win are the lawyers. They make the money and many times you walk away with nothing but a huge nightmare and a broken family.

This is why wills and trusts, as well as incorporating your company, can be so important to protecting yourself and your family. These are legal documents that will ensure your wishes are met, when you are no longer able to speak for yourself or if someone feels you wronged them in some kind of way and seeks payback.

You know Granny, she is always on top of her finances. Granny Frumpy replied "Boy, you better believe it, Granny Frumpy won't let any of my money make people act funny."

She went on to say that she and Grandpa Frumpy had drawn up their wills and also set up a living trust years ago, but recently had to update them because of their son Fred's sudden death.

Granny Frumpy's will has a list of her belongings such as jewelry and antiques that would be distributed to her closest relatives.

She has also set up an "Irrevocable Trust," which includes all of her real estate, life insurance and some investments within.

Granny Frumpy wants to make sure that all that

she has gained from her hard work will last for many generations. Of course, she does not want to give money to Uncle Sam, the one she really doesn't like. Nothing gets by Granny Frumpy, she is as frugal as they come and probably why she has been so successful all these years.

Her "Star Team" of advisors helped her evaluate all her wishes and decided to set up her family trust.

Frank asked Granny if she could do a video like Fred Frumpy did, to serve as a message of life for her family.

She said she already did one and it was her idea that Fred did one too.

Granny Frumpy says "When you do a video, the only thing the attorneys, courts or family members can argue is that you were not in your right mind when you did it."

Granny probably made sure that no one she mentioned in her video could twist her words or thoughts, especially since they know she loves her weekly glass of wine.

She believes what it is most important, is leaving behind the real values of life: integrity, honesty, hard work, caring and love. It's important to have a big heart and to always remember that life is only a passage, so enjoy the trip.

Chapter XXVI

Estate Planning

"By failing to prepare, you are preparing to fail."
Benjamin Franklin

It has often been said that there are only two things in life that are for sure: death and taxes. So there is a 100% chance you will live your life paying taxes and die, still paying taxes.

What is an Estate?

Everyone owns something at death, whether it be a car, computer, jewelry, clothing, furnishings, real estate, investments, cash or all of the above. These belongings are your "estate" and they need to be directed somewhere or to someone at the time of your death.

Why Estate Planning?

Rich or poor, young or old, when you die, you leave behind an estate.

Green Nugget: "MONEY MAKES PEOPLE ACT FUNNY."

The more money that is included in your estate, the more your family and their attorneys will want it. I have seen the best of family relationships crumble because of money, it is very sad but there are thousands of stories that make it FACT.

Do you really want your family fighting over your gold necklace, or that funny looking artwork on your wall?

How about having taxes or attorney's fees and probate courts "eat up" your entire nest egg or lifelong savings earned from all of that hard work. Like most people, you would rather have peace of mind that your loved ones can enjoy it or put it to better use for future generations.

Example: If you were to die without a will (or "intestate," in legalese), state law will determine how most of your belongings are distributed, and it may not be the way you wanted.

You have worked so hard to buy your home, to build your business and to save for retirement, surely you want to make sure that everything is protected and in the right place when you die, so your wishes are honored.

You might be thinking, "wait a minute, you mean to tell me I am going to die?" No you are not going to die; you are going to live forever. So forget setting up an estate plan. However, for those of you that understand the day will come and how sudden it can happen, you should be prepared. Why not make things as easy as possible for your family?

Estate plans help you and your family avoid unnecessary taxes, high probate costs and attorney fees, as well as long delays. And when I say long delays I mean LONG! Sometimes it can be years before your estate will be settled, all because you didn't put your estate plan in place.

If you want to protect your assets you should have an estate plan and a financial plan in place, this way your family's assets will be protected for the many generations you will leave behind.

So... now you understand why you need an estate plan?

Green Nugget: Don't think, just because you don't have assets that you don't need to have these basic documents in place. No matter your net worth, it is important for everyone to have these documents in place, so at least you will know when the time comes, your wishes will come true, and no one can say otherwise.

Estate plans are generally comprised of:

- A will – Which you have already learned about!
- A power of attorney
- A trust
- A living will or medical power of attorney

A living will is not the same thing as a durable medical power of attorney.

A living will makes your wishes known when it comes to life prolonging medical treatments, and it takes the form of a directive.

A durable medical power of attorney authorizes another party to make medical decisions for you (including end-of-life decisions) if you become incapacitated or otherwise unable to make these decisions.

Now that you have set up an estate plan, that does not mean you are all set!

You should review it and keep it up to date, because things are certain to change in your life.

You may purchase new properties, get married again, have children, grandchildren; laws may change as well and so too will the need for your estate plan to change along with them.

On the next page fill out the Estate Planning Table.

Estate Planning Checklist	yes	no	notes
I have a will			
I have a trust			
I have not moved to a different state since last reviewing my trust and/or will.			
My marital status has not changed since I last reviewed my trust and/or will.			
I have taken the steps necessary to suggest a guardian for my minor child(ren) or other dependents, should this be necessary.			
I have no additional children or grandchildren since my trust and/or will were last reviewed.			
My children and/or spouse would need no assistance in managing property left to them by me.			
I have not experienced a significant increase or decrease in wealth since my last estate planning review.			
I have not given away or sold property that is designated to go to an heir.			
My special friends have been provided for in my estate plan.			
Everyone I have provided for in previous plans still needs the same amount and type of assistance.			
I have made adequate provisions for transferring business interests I may own.			
There are no persons for whom I would like to provide temporary help (e.g. education of children)and/or grand-children or supplement parents' retirement resources).			
I am aware of the amount of property I may leave tax-free under current federal and state law.			
I have a good idea of the amount of estate taxes that will be due at my death and have specified how each heir's share should be reduced as a result.			
I am confident that the life insurance coverage I have is both necessary and adequate for the support of loved ones, payment of taxes (if applicable), and other estate settlement expenses.			
I am aware that it is necessary to designate beneficiaries for any balances remaining in my retirement accounts.			

Estate Planning Checklist	yes	no	notes
I have ensured that proper beneficiary forms have been completed and are up to date.			
The person I have chosen to handle my estate settlement is still willing and able to serve.			
I have ensured that proper beneficiary forms have been completed and are up to date.			
The person I have chosen to handle my estate settlement is still willing and able to serve.			
I am relying on joint ownership arrangements to handle some of my estate planning needs.			
I am aware that all professional advisors (attorneys, accountants, etc.) can furnish fee estimates upon request.			
My financial records are easily accessible and readily understandable.			
I have made a valid written Advance Health Care Directive and have duly appointed my agent to carry out my instructions in the event I can not make healthcare decisions on my own behalf.			
I have made my funeral and burial wishes known to my loved ones.			
I am aware that under some circumstances my heirs will not be allowed to remove the contents of my safe deposit box without court supervision.			
The charitable causes and institutions I support are remembered in my estate plan as I wish.			
I realize that by planning properly, it is possible to reduce estate settlement costs.			

It may sound very complex, but remember to always ask questions or address concerns that come to mind with your financial advisor and your attorney. They will work together to make things a lot easier for you and give you peace of mind.

Hopefully, by now you have your "Star Team" of professionals that you can trust. Just make sure you always ask questions and do your own homework, don't ever think they are always up to date on the laws and changes that come each year.

Now that you understand the whole concept of having an estate plan, you can avoid ending up like some of these folks:

- Joseph Robbie –owner of the Miami Dolphins owed $45 million in estate taxes

- Conrad Hilton- creator of the largest and most profitable hotel empire owed over $100 million in estate taxes

- Jacqueline Kennedy Onassis - owed $23 million in estate taxes, yet hired some of the world's finest tax planners.

- George Steinbrenner - owner of the New York Yankees, may be the most classic of all stories. Mr. Steinbrenner owed $0 in Federal estate taxes because of a tax loophole when he died in 2010, that is still in question and may still be changed in the future, who knows?

How about those Joneses who have not spoken to each other in years because their grandpa never had a will and his estate has been in probate courts for the last five years? To make matter worse, each family's different attorneys keep dragging out the process more and more with thousands of dollars in attorneys' fees owed.

Let's see how the Frumpys handle all this.

Fran Frumpy wrote in her will that Fonzie will be given to Flavia and Fabio (Uncle Floyd's twin boys). Fonzie really enjoys jumping around their crib! He runs around, he barks and is very protective of his cousins.

Fran's Will

Fonzie goes to Uncle Floyd's kids

Fouis Futton handbags to Auntie Frida

Fartier earrings to Momma Flo

Retirement plan beneficiaries are Frank & Momma Flo

Life Insurance beneficiaries are Frank and Momma Flo...yes...Fonzie also is listed

Shoe collection goes to Fofina

You don't need to be rich and famous to do estate planning. We all have an estate, all of our wishes will differ and most likely will those of the loved ones you leave behind, so don't let anyone come in between what's most important, YOUR wishes.

Human nature tends to make us procrastinate and say I will get to it another day. That's the easy way out, to let it be someone else's problem to deal with.

Do not wait until you get sick, or have kids, or see your friend come down with a terrible illness or suffer an accident, or you decide to go on some adventurous long trip to the Amazon that you might not come back from.

Make today a day of action, so that you can live everyday knowing your wishes in life be cherished forever.

Do it for you... and do it for your family.

Then you can die in peace! Unless you want to see your loved ones struggle, that is.

Green Nugget: Consider doing an audio and video recording outlining your wishes. This will help prevent anyone from arguing or trying to misinterpret your wishes, the legal system can always find loop holes it seems. The last thing you want is that son or daughter-in law you never liked, running off with your families inheritance... your legacy.

Keep it in a safe place along with your will or important documents regarding your final wishes.

Chapter XXVII

Realities of Long Term Care

"In youth we run into difficulties; in old age difficulties run into us."
Josh Billings

You may have a grandma or grandpa living with you or you might have a family member taking care of grandpa now, or maybe grandma is taking care of grandpa in their own home. Maybe you have a neighbor that cares for a father or mother or son or daughter.

Everybody knows someone that is or had to take care of a loved one at some point in their lives. If you have never been through it, ask someone who has at some point or is going through it right now, it's not easy, but they will tell you, "You just do it."

Long Term Care: is the care you need when you are no longer able to care for yourself. It is the type of personal care required when we are unable to take care of the normal activities we take for granted, such as eating, bathing, dressing, toileting, moving around, maintaining continence, or simply in need of guidance for safety purposes due to cognitive impairment or dementia. This type of care requires assistance over a long period of time, often times for the rest of your life.

Long term care can range from simple assistance in your own home, to assistance required in a residential care facility (aka assisted living community), to that of an adult day care center, or it may require more highly skilled care in that of a nursing home setting.

Typically long term care is not covered by your health

insurance, HMO, Medicare or supplemental policies. These types of policies are designed to only pay for short-term care not long term care. They are designed to cover surgeries, doctor visits, medicines, rehabilitative needs and so on, anything you can relate to the first three months of care, after that you are on your own.

That's right, after three months, you are now considered in need of long term care services, and you are on your own to pay for it out of pocket.

I know a friend whose mom had to care for her husband until he passed away. The problem was that he needed her help for four years and she barely had the time to take care of herself. I have heard so many stories that I could talk for hours, just imagine having to care for a loved one.

My favorite statement is, "My kids will take care of me."

Really?

Do you really think your kids will take care of you? Do you really want your kids caring for you?

Another great statement I have heard over the years, "the government will take care of me."

Really?

Have you looked at our national debt lately? Or your state's debt? Let's think about this one for a minute.

Facts:

- 70 million Baby boomers

- 50% of the people will need long term care at some point in their lives

- In 2011 the cost of care in a nursing home, national average: $75,000-$130,000 per year

- Average stay in a nursing home: 2.5 years
- 85% of the people that need care stay in their own home or assisted living before entering a nursing home

To all of our politicians, to our media analysts, to all our taxpayers, to all of my friends and for the love of this country, DO THE MATH AND WAKE UP!

Talk about 800 pound gorilla that no one wants to address. Do the MATH!

WE THE PEOPLE CAN NOT AFFORD THE COST OF CARE ANYMORE!

Add on top of that, thanks to EDUCATION and TECHNOLOGY we ALL are going to now LIVE LONGER, thus making the need for care more of a REALITY for all of us.

In our society, we see how magical it is to be young and healthy. But all of us are going to get older someday. Unfortunately how many of us are not prepared for it?

Let's stop, because this is not just an OLD AGE issue.

Forty percent of those in need of long term care services are under the age of 65.

Let's do the math here...

Let's say 10 years from now:

70 million baby boomers = 50% will need care = 35 million people X only 15% will get to a nursing home situation = average cost of NHC in 2020 per year $100,000 =

Half a TRILLION dollars will be spent on long term illness/ care per YEAR by either YOU or tax payers.

$525,000,000,000 per year!

If you want to argue with my numbers, do you really think I didn't pad the numbers (make them as conservative as possible)? I love numbers, and let me tell you, my numbers are NOT RIGHT at all, because they are WAY TOO CONSERVATIVE.

Three in four Americans will need long term care services but are not prepared to pay for them. And these services, which can cost thousands of dollars, are not covered by traditional insurance or Medicare.

Assisted-living prices run about $3,000 a month. A nursing home is a staggering $8,000 a month on average.

Think with me now: if you need long term care at some point of your life, the cost of long term care will wipe out all your retirement, your savings...everything.

Besides that, do you want to be a burden to your family? They probably don't even have the time for all of that, they have their own lives, jobs, kids, or just trying to stay afloat in today's economy to pay their own bills.

How can you be prepared?

This book is about solutions, once we know the problems that are out there, you must focus on the solutions for your life.

Educate yourself and your family, have this **important discussion** that no one wants to have. Now, it won't be fun and most likely won't go anywhere, because for you or your loved one it won't happen to you, right?

It is time to get real. Evaluate what your options are, just in case you or a loved one is to need long term care one day.

Research the cost. Check the cost of a long term care facility or service provider in your city or a place you feel you will most likely consider locating should you need long term care, maybe closer to your loved ones, who would be in the best position to provide the necessary care and all the responsibilities that come with it, including driving to the doctor, meeting with specialists, hiring aides (or firing aides), interviewing facilities, finding a facility that has availability, researching financial history, gathering all documents, filling out all documents, working with social services to have the state subsidize costs, going through years of financial statements to make sure there were no illegal transfers, staying up all night or changing shifts with the care taker, being able to be there if an aid doesn't show up or something goes wrong in the facility you choose, provide transportation when needed...list goes on, am I making my point yet?

Don't be naïve and think, "The good Lord is going to take care of me."

The good Lord gave you choices in life, what would the Pope have said who suffered from Parkinson's, or Ronald Reagan who suffered from Alzheimer's, or Superman who fell off a horse and was paralyzed...the list goes on, we are all equal when it comes to our health. No one is invincible.

Everyone needs to have a strategy for addressing the potential problems associated with long term care expenses and the burden that is often placed on loved ones to struggle with.

The earlier you plan, the better.

When you plan ahead you may also be able to protect your assets instead of having to use them all to pay for your care, leaving nothing left behind for a spouse, children, family and charities.

Long Term Care Insurance:

This insurance pays for the costs associated with skilled, intermediate or custodial care. Long term care insurance is designed to pay for care that is going to be needed for a long period of time. This type of insurance will pay for home care costs, assisted living facility costs, adult day care costs or nursing home costs.

Most people do not ever want to live in a nursing home, however, based on your assets and income and your states laws, long term care insurance may be the only way for your family to keep you out of nursing home.

Many people think long term care insurance is too expensive, but how expensive is one month in a nursing home facility or long term care setting like an assisted living or to pay nurses to come and help you and your family in your own home?

Just three months of paying for a nursing home can make a significant dent into your retirement, assets and savings. Imagine what just one year's worth of care can do.

I have seen multi-millionaires pay $10,000 per month for a parent, and even $20,000 per month for both. I don't care how much money you think you have or don't have, no one wants to spend 10-20 thousand dollars per month, period! Not even our rock stars and celebs enjoy doing that on Rodeo Drive in Hollywood every month, it gets old. Now think about not having to pay that cost, but instead having to care for a loved one 24 hours a day, seven days week. I have a good friend, who I can't say enough positive things about, that is caring for his parents everyday he wakes, that is his job. You may have loved ones doing the same, talk about patience and strength.

What about all our heroes coming home from war? The men and women that put their lives on the line for our freedoms, think about the many that will need help and assistance for maybe the rest of their lives?

We must begin to have this discussion, the time is now, and we don't have time to waste anymore.

Do NOT rely on the government to fix this serious problem we, as a country, are about to face. They have come up with some ridiculous legislation as answers in the past and will throw more money at the problems...money we don't have right?

I won't go any further into this discussion, instead go do your homework to help you make a change for the better. The situation is not even laughable, it is outright SAD that so many people have not had the opportunity or the time to plan or maybe they believed the government was going to be their savior.

I want to stress to you that long term care expenses can wipe out your savings, and everything else you have worked hard to establish so quickly that it's beyond scary. However, what's scarier is that not everyone can qualify for insurance. It is very difficult to get.

Long term care insurance, when properly purchased, can help you avoid all of your fears about losing everything you've worked your entire life for, and more importantly it can greatly reduce the burden placed on your family and friends.

Some states have a partnership plan for long term which is a program that combines private long term care insurance and Medicaid extended coverage.

Make sure you always speak to your financial adviser or a professional who specializes in long term care planning; he or she can give you a better idea of the costs and financial strategies that may be suitable for your situation.

Long term care insurance is not as expensive as you think;

evaluate your options when you are young and healthy (60 years of age and below). Don't let those foolish articles tell you that you have enough money that you don't have to worry about it or that you are too young to buy long term care insurance. We have so many scenarios and different stories to share, that is why it is most important that you know your own unique situation and what matters to you most.

Is it protecting loved ones?

Is it protecting assets?

Is it being in full control of your care, should you need it?

Is it making sure you've given yourself enough options so you never have to go to a nursing home?

Or is it simply, that you never want to put the burden upon a loved one, or for them to have to go through the necessary paperwork involved, or providing you care, or dealing with aides or facilities, or other family members...the list goes on and on.

Just ask someone who's going through it now like a family member or the neighbor or friend that is caring for their spouse or loved one.

If you don't know of anyone, ask around, I am sure that someone knows someone that would be more than happy to share their story, in hopes you will do all you can to never have to go through what they have.

Green Nugget: Just because you can't afford, or qualify, or believe in insurance, doesn't mean you have NO OPTIONS. What it really means, is that you need to work with the right professionals, like an elder law attorney and financial advisor or planner who specializes in estate and/or long term care planning to design the most appropriate plan possible.

"You do not need to be afraid of getting old. You just need to be prepared." That's what Fred Frumpy used to say to his parents.

Fred was the one that made sure Grandpa and Granny Frumpy purchased long term care insurance.

Granny and Grandpa said they would not need it. They said they had enough money to pay for the care if they ever needed it.

You know how Grandpa is. When he thinks he is right, you can't disagree with him, he is ALWAYS RIGHT. I'm sure you might know someone like that, or sometimes like that yourself.

So, Fred spoke to Granny, and told her his family would not be able to take care of them if they were to get sick or need long term care. Flo, Frank, Uncle Floyd and Auntie Frida all they have their own lives and their own "Napkin on the Fridge." They have their own problems and do not have time to be a nurse. Really, do you think Uncle Floyd would bathe or clean up Granny after going to the bathroom?

Yes, they love Grandpa and Granny Frumpy, but they can't put off their lives to start managing drugs, giving baths or running to and from the pharmacy. It is a hard thing to put on anyone, especially your loved ones.

Nobody knows what life will bring.

Besides, when you have long term care insurance, you can pick the best treatment, the best care, the best facilities, and hopefully stay out of nursing home as long as possible, hopefully forever.

After Grandpa Frumpy visited one of his buddies in the nursing home, the only thing he could smell for weeks was his buddy's stinky room. Grandpa Frumpy said his buddy was just another number, and said the nurses forgot about what his buddy did in his pants that day he went to see him!

That's when Grandpa Frumpy agreed that getting the insurance made sense; I guess he was right in the end, as always.

Grandpa Frumpy is a very proud man, so the last thing he could envision in life would be to have his family take care of him. Though there was one thing Granny Frumpy knew about her hubby, and that was that he would never want to lose his dignity.

It would kill him to know that because of his stubbornness about long term care insurance that he would let all those years she beat him over the head with her favorite pot, go to waste. It would also kill him to know that all of their life savings were wiped out and his final days would be covered by the government. Granny Frumpy is one savvy woman, as you know, and she probably beat him over the head a few times making sure they bought the insurance whether he liked it or not, which was really for his own good.

Or maybe she has a little bit of Uncle Floyd in her, and the last thing she wanted in her life was to clean up after Grandpa Frumpy. She always made sure he has his "man time" in the mornings for good reason, especially because he loves his spicy food... ugh!

That's when Granny said to Fred: "Son, you are so right! I want to keep my dignity and a clean place to be in when the days I need care come about. It would be great to have a nice nurse to take care of me when I need it. And if I never need care, you know, your dad Grandpa Frumpy is a wonderful father and husband, but he can barely take care of himself, so how's he going to take care of me?"

Granny also knew all their assets would be protected by having a long term care insurance policy. But most importantly, she knows it would allow her to keep her independence.

Grandpa agreed. He might be stubborn, but those who know him well know he married Granny for a reason. Grandpa Frumpy is no dummy, nor would he ever be selfish enough to allow his family to take care of him if there was a way that he could prevent it.

Chapter XXVIII

Live Life to the Fullest

Too often we go through life on autopilot, going through the motions and having each day pass like the one before it.

We wake up, we go to work, we sleep, and we wake up again and then it's back to the grind day in and day out.

It isn't until something big happens, and it changes the way you see your life.

Hopefully by getting to this page there was at least one green nugget along the way that will help prepare you differently for that something or get you motivated to start changing your ways today.

Let your I-Plan be your guide during your exciting journey to financial freedom.

You can and WILL SUCCEED, no matter how high the mountain seems to be. With belief, passion, education and that all important will power, no person or obstacle that gets thrown in your way will be able to stop you.

Thank you again to all our HEROES who proudly served and fought for our freedom.

Let's make them, and those that came before them proud, by achieving our FINANCIAL FREEDOM.

Make it happen!!!

m$m

I bet you're wondering what happened to The Frumpys? They are all together today. It's Thanksgiving and they have so much to be thankful for.

They are thankful for their health. They are thankful they are together as a family because that is what really matters in life, the moments we share.

They are thankful that they have a lot good people surrounding them that are helping them achieve their dreams.

They are thankful to have had Fred in their lives. He will be forever in their memories.

Granny Frumpy took her book and peacefully read the words as Fonzie laid on her feet with his bone:

If I Had My Life to Live Over
I'd dare to make more mistakes next time.
I'd relax, I would limber up.
I would be sillier than I have been during this trip
I would take fewer things seriously
I would take more chances
I would climb more mountains and swim more rivers
I would eat more ice cream and less beans
I would perhaps have more actual troubles,
But I'd have few imaginary ones
You see, I'm one of those people who live sensibly
And sanely hour after hour, day after day
Oh, I've had my moments
And if I had it to do over again,
I'd have more of them
In fact, I'd try to have nothing else
Just moments, one after another,
Instead of living so many years ahead of each day
I've been one of those persons who never
Goes anywhere without a thermometer,
A hot water bottle, a raincoat and a parachute.
If I had to do it again,
I would travel lighter than I have
If I had my life to live over,
I would start barefoot earlier in the spring
And stay that way later in the fall
I would go to more dances,
I would ride more merry-go-rounds.
I would pick more daisies.
The Frumpy family together understood the message. Live it to
the fullest. Be in charge of your life. You are the only one that can
change it, if you do not like it.

It is your trip and you can and will SUCCEED.
Just believe in your I-Plan!

Success is not a journey, it is DESTINY.

To all of our Angels

Life is risky sometimes
But really, you gotta take your chances
Stay with me, don't fall sleep too soon
The angels can wait for a moment.

Author: Michael G. Minter
Co-Creator: Anelise Minter
Publisher: Mintco Financial, Inc.
Editor: Jaclyn Castek
Illustrations: Gloria Minter
Cover and Layout Design: Erik Minter